T5-AWE-973

Effective English Teaching

CEE Commission on Research in Teacher Effectiveness

William H. Peters, Chair, Texas A&M University
Faye Louise Grindstaff, California State University, Northridge
Richard L. Hanzelka, Mississippi Bend Area Education Agency
Miles C. Olson, University of Colorado at Boulder

Effective English Teaching

Concept, Research, and Practice

William H. Peters, Chair,
and the CEE Commission on Research
in Teacher Effectiveness

National Council of Teachers of English
1111 Kenyon Road, Urbana, Illinois 61801

NCTE Editorial Board: Candy Carter, Lee Galda-Pellegrini, Donald R. Gallo, Delores Lipscomb, Thomas Newkirk; L. Jane Christensen, *ex officio*

Staff Editor: Tim Bryant

Interior Book Design: Tom Kovacs for TGK Design

NCTE Stock Number 12935

© 1987 by the National Council of Teachers of English. All rights reserved. Printed in the United States of America.

It is the policy of NCTE in its journals and other publications to provide a forum for the open discussion of ideas concerning the content and the teaching of English and the language arts. Publicity accorded to any particular point of view does not imply endorsement by the Executive Committee, the Board of Directors, or the membership at large, except in announcements of policy, where such endorsement is clearly specified.

Library of Congress Cataloging-in-Publication Data

Effective English teaching.

  Includes bibliographies.
  1. English language—Study and teaching (Elementary)—
United States.   I. Peters, William H., 1933–   .
II. CEE Commission on Research in Teacher Effectiveness.
LB1576.E33   1987   372.6'1   87-22018
ISBN 0-8141-1293-5

Contents

Preface

The Conference on English Education Commission on Research in Teacher Effectiveness was given a threefold charge: to review research relevant to teacher effectiveness, report commission findings, and make recommendations based on the research literature. In response to this charge, commission members made an extensive search of the teacher effectiveness research. Their findings support an observation that James Squire (1969) made: "Certainly we must admit that strong academic preparation, in its conventional sense at least, does not alone help teachers to cope with the realities of the classroom. . . . Too seldom in reforming teacher education have we moved much beyond academic competence as a goal." (5) The central dilemma of American English education, as Squire saw it, has yet to be resolved: how to prepare today's teachers to face realistically, but with enthusiasm and insight, the harsh realities of our classrooms.

In this report, we will present essential information drawn from the research in teacher effectiveness. Presented within the context of an organic field model of the teaching of English, the discussion is designed to help both pre-service and in-service teachers to understand the realities of today's classrooms and become more effective English teachers. In a recent article, Moffett (1985) argues that curriculum improvement is blocked by "a set of attitudes and emotions in both the public and the profession that is mostly unconscious." (52) It is hoped that the commission's report will help remove these impediments and improve teaching effectiveness in English language arts.

William H. Peters, Chair
CEE Commission on Research in Teacher Effectiveness

References

Moffett, J. 1985. Hidden Impediments to Improving English Teaching. *Phi Delta Kappan* 67:50–56.
Squire, J. R. 1969. The New Responsibilities of English Education. *English Education* 1:5–11.

Note: Chapters 2–5 of this text are each followed by a list of references. Documents indexed in *Resources in Education (RIE)* are denoted by a 6-digit ED (ERIC Document) number. The majority of ERIC documents are reproduced on microfiche and may be viewed at ERIC collections in libraries and other institutions or can be ordered from the ERIC Document Reproduction Service (EDRS) in either paper copy or microfiche. For ordering information and price schedules write or call EDRS, 3900 Wheeler Avenue, Alexandria, VA 22304, 1-800-227-3742.

Introduction

Effective English Teaching: Concept, Research, and Practice presents a model that allows us to look beyond academic competence as the be-all and end-all of effective English teaching. The report enables us to see the teaching of English and the training of English teachers for the fascinating world it is.

For far too long, with a repetition that rings of cant, we have been told that all a good teacher needs to know is the subject matter. While it would be folly to deny that teachers must have a command of the subject matter, too often the dynamics of working in a classroom with students have been ignored in the rush to emphasize content without method and context, teaching without learning.

The 1986 NCTE *Guidelines for the Preparation of Teachers of English Language Arts* identifies factors that have emerged since the 1976 *Statement on the Preparation of Teachers of English and the Language Arts.* The 1986 report includes a section on attitudes, which attends to concern for students, adaptability, and professional perspective. Authoring the 1986 guidelines, the NCTE Standing Committee on Teacher Preparation and Certification expressed its concern that pre-service teachers "see teaching as a dynamic profession rather than as a static activity." *Effective English Teaching* directly addresses this concern.

The organic field model of teaching English presented in this monograph offers a new and dynamic view of the interactions that occur in the classroom. Seeing this model as a sphere in constant flux, rather than as a flat circle, allows us to realize in a new and exciting manner what we do when we teach English. The often-felt split between English, education, and English education is smoothed and repaired by this model. The *substance* of what we teach—using the familiar tripod of language, literature, and composition—must overlap with the *skills* of listening, reading, writing, and speaking embodied in the communications skills model. Even these aspects of what we do cannot be seen without viewing how they overlap with the *process,* be it affective, cognitive, or creative.

By introducing the *context* of community, policy, and profession into the model, this monograph presents us with the range of choices we make in teaching English. The model makes us aware that the teaching of

1

English occurs when process, substance, and skills unite in a particular and realized context.

Teaching English and training English teachers are amazingly complex and complicated undertakings. Those of us who have worked in the field for many years know this. Those who are new to the field also know this. Aided by the organic field model of teaching English, we can begin to realize the range and parameters of our discipline. This "speculative instrument," as I. A. Richards would term it, opens new vistas for us to contemplate and new avenues of research. The vast amount of recent and important research gathered from many areas other than English education to support the model is in itself enough to make this text a valuable reference. Educators who work in the pre-service and in-service education of English teachers, as well as those in curriculum development and supervision, will find this book a useful tool.

In particular, the chapter on context in teaching brings together research on many variables that we know affect student performance. Instinctively we have recognized the effects of the contexts of school, community, home, socioeconomic status, parental attitude, administration, class size, and homogeneity. But here we find help in understanding the complex interplay of these variables and help in raising questions so that we can penetrate the enormity of our task.

In recent years, the field of English education has become fragmented through specialization, which makes an overview difficult. Literature, composition, language, rhetoric, adolescent literature, grammar, methods, testing, evaluation, research, and many other areas vie for our attention and specialization. *Effective English Teaching* gives us the overview that has been lacking in our publications and in our work.

Bruce C. Appleby
Southern Illinois University at Carbondale
Chair, Conference on English Education, 1987

I An Organic Field Model of the Teaching of English

A major problem in research on teaching has been the absence of models that define the context and content variables constraining teaching decisions. This chapter presents a model for teaching English that attempts to define these broader dimensions and provides a frame of reference through which one may view factors limiting the English teacher's choices. To reflect a complete picture, studies that report research on teaching in general should refer to this model or a similar one when applying those findings to the specifics of English.

Dimensions of the Model

Defining the discipline of English in operational terms has always been difficult, and the difficulty may be one of the reasons for the paucity of specific research on teaching English. Most colleges and universities tend to act as if English were primarily the study of literature. On the other hand, many elementary schools seem to view English as merely the study of grammar. Clearly, considerable confusion exists, at least in practice, as to what English is. Although many attempts have been made to define the discipline, innumerable scholars have relied on the "tripod" of language, literature, and composition for defining the subject matter of English.

Merely defining the content of our discipline is not enough, however: English educators must also describe its *teaching*. We labor under a nagging suspicion that English teaching is somehow different from other teaching. That further dimension causes even greater concern.

English is a complex discipline, and therefore many differing views abound concerning the nature of the field as well as its teaching. The model presented here provides a basis for study. It will assist practitioner and researcher alike.

According to the organic field model, the teaching of English is constrained by at least two major sets of variables: content and context. The *content* variables are substance, skills, and process. The *context* variables involve community, policy, and profession. The following outline adds subordinate dimensions to the primary variables.

3

Content Variables

I. Substance
    A. Literature
    B. Language
    C. Rhetoric
II. Skills
    A. Reading
    B. Writing
    C. Listening
    D. Speaking
III. Process
    A. Affective
    B. Cognitive
    C. Creative

Context Variables

I. Community
    A. Social-psychological
    B. Economic
    C. Linguistic
II. Policy
    A. Human
    B. Legal
    C. Fiscal
    D. Physical
III. Profession
    A. Teacher
        1. Personal
        2. Academic
        3. Experiential
    B. Department
        1. Philosophy
        2. Goals
        3. Practices
            a. Personal
            b. Curricular
            c. Administrative
            d. Pedagogical
    C. The larger profession
        1. Theories
        2. Traditions
        3. Practices in vogue

Each of these variables relates to the teaching of English; in combination and in interaction, they define the teaching dimension of the discipline. Scholars will of course continue to emphasize the separate components in their analytic studies of the content of English. However, the general view of what constrains the teaching of English must be broader, more multidimensional. The model provides a frame of reference for that conception of the English teacher's craft (Figure 1, next page).

The Content Variable

Consider first the three content dimensions of substance, skills, and process and their interconnectedness. Most educators would probably agree that these three dimensions must interact in some way for English teaching to happen. For example, it would be difficult to teach literature or language or rhetoric without some reading, writing, listening, or speaking. Similarly, the study of any substantive area in English cannot occur without some cognitive, affective, or creative activity.

The model carries this matter a step further, however. It posits that under the best conditions every unit of instruction in English should include *each* of the content subcategories. Each unit should include some emphasis on all three substantive areas of literature, language, and rhetoric. One dimension will typically predominate, with the others in supporting roles. But each should be there.

Similarly, each of the four skills—reading, writing, listening, and speaking—should also come into play during any given unit of instruction. Attempts to improve students' use of these skills should always be made in the context of the substance of English. One must read something when learning to read. In English class, that "something" should be the substance of English.

Finally, the process variable should also be given attention in each unit of instruction. The teacher should help students develop the ability to think, to value, and to create. But this instruction should be given within the context of the skills and substance of English. Thinking, valuing, and creating cannot be taught in isolation from skills and substance. In English, the skills and substance of the discipline are the vehicles through which the process variables are taught.

Many would say that the skills and process variables are shared directly by other disciplines, but that the substance variable with its subcategories of literature, language, and rhetoric is unique to English. One might thus say that, for most persons, substance defines our discipline and shapes the ways in which we teach skills and process.

However, other disciplines use the substance of English, too. For example, a history teacher might use historical fiction, biography, or even

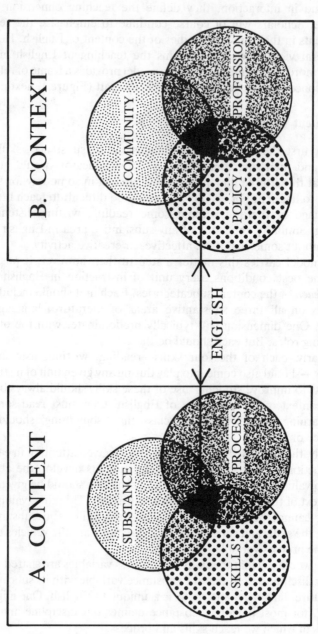

Figure 1. Organic field model of teaching English, showing the relationship between content variables (A) and context variables (B).

poetry to illumine the study of an event or period of history. Thus, not substance alone, but our particular *use* of substance, defines English teaching through our emphasis on the other variables. For instruction, we often set goals that relate to values (the affective side of the process variable), especially as those values can be inferred from literature or language or rhetoric. We also hope that our students will learn to evaluate what they read, hear, and say (the cognitive dimension). And of course we often have students learn through creating the very forms they are studying—something quite uncommon in other disciplines.

So we might say that what we practice is defined by substance and process. However, is not our approach to skills also unique? It seems to be, at least insofar as the skills are conditioned by our substance and our process. Literature and science are not read in the same way. One listens for different things in English class than in mathematics class. Especially when interpreting poetry and drama, one uses different speaking skills in an English class than in an art class. Much of the writing for an English class will be different in form and style than the writing for a history class.

Can we say that English is completely different from other disciplines? Of course not. But English *is* different, and not merely because the substance is different. The difference lies in our approach to skills and process.

In summary, English is taught when, and only when, the particular substance, skills, and process variables listed here come together. When only one or two categories appear in a lesson, it is not truly English teaching—at least as defined by this model.

An Extended Application of the Content Portion

We have seen how the model shows the three category variables coming together in the classroom to shape the teaching of English. Given that definition, the effective application of the discipline extends one level deeper. Consider a literature-centered lesson, say the study of a short story. If the class is to be truly an English class, the teacher would have to involve students in skills and process activities as well as in those activities directly related to the substance (the literary selection) being taught.

Extending the Substance

Would not the instruction be more effective if the teacher were to include language study, something relating to semantics or style, as a part of the substance of the lesson? The students might derive a more complete sense of the literary work if the teacher were to include such study.

Would not the students also profit from some rhetoric-based study in approaching the literary work? Synthesizing their understanding of the rhetorical purposes and effects of the work, comparing its form with other works, summarizing a discussion of the work—with each of these activities taking place within a rhetorical-compositional context—would surely expand the students' understanding of the selection.

Extending the Skills

The many dimensions of the skills category should be considered as well. Typically a teacher engages students in reading and listening. Would it not make the experience more complete if the students were also engaged in writing and speaking?

Extending the Process

A teacher might concentrate heavily on the cognitive dimension of the process category, say through a careful analysis of the plot of the short story or through a criterion-based evaluation of the work. But what if the teacher were to make a connection between the story and the students' experiences (the affective dimension) or to ask students to create a narrative poem around the plot of the story (the creative dimension)? Again, the experience would probably be more complete.

Summary of the Content Portion

The organic field model suggests that English is taught most completely and effectively when substance, skills, and process come together in a classroom. The model also suggests the need to include (albeit with varying degrees of emphasis) literature, language, and rhetoric in each unit of instruction. The skills of reading, writing, listening, and speaking similarly should be employed to foster competence in the skill areas and to exploit all possible modes of information processing. Finally, the cognitive, affective, and creative processes should be employed in every unit to develop intellectual strategies and to foster substantive learning. English is best taught when these variables interact with and complement one another in the instructional context. The result is a multidimensional opportunity for student learning.

The Context Variable

The context of English is similar to that of every other discipline, except in its specifics and their application. Context strongly influences what the teacher does in the classroom. Community, policy, and profession variables shape both the choices available to teachers and their options for responding (see again Figure 1).

The Community

Because American education has traditionally been a function of the local community, the norms and values of that community naturally affect what happens in the classroom. Normally, informal local values and expectations, rather than the formal decisions of a board of education, most influence what occurs in the classroom.

The Social-Psychological Dimension

Consider first the community's collective personal norms and values. If a school population is made up of students whose mean IQ is 120, a teacher has a quite different set of options than if the mean IQ were a more normal 100. Thus the students' *abilities* strongly shape the choices that teachers make. This value may hold true at the broader community level as well. In communities of well-educated people, parents are apt to assume that learning is as easy for all students as it was for them. Such a community will often expect the basics to be covered rapidly and require advanced study of all students.

Students' *experiences* also shape instruction. If the students have a wide diversity of experiences, a teacher may decide to pursue a historical rather than a thematic study of literature. For a thematic approach to be effective, the organizing themes must be selected on the basis of the students' common experiences. Community experiences also influence teaching possibilities; parents' experiences constrain teachers' choices as well. Parents commonly expect their children to have the same educational experiences they had. The pervasive influence of tradition is illustrated by our present study of grammar, mechanics, spelling, and vocabulary in isolation from composition as a means of influencing correctness in writing.

The collective *interests* of students limit what teachers may do in classrooms. Good teachers know that they must make their disciplines relevant to the lives of their students if the study of those disciplines is to be worthwhile. Students tend to pass through similar predictable physiological stages, thus providing an important reference point for the teacher. One would think, therefore, that teachers should make teaching decisions based on this reasonably predictable variable. Yet community pressures often interfere with curriculum planning based on these student characteristics. It is unusual, for example, for a community to support the use of adolescent literature in the English class even though it may be the most appropriate for the developing adolescent. Thus the community's interests and those of the students are often at odds; as a result, the teacher's choices are limited. The teacher is challenged to find procedures and materials that fit the contextual constraints of students and community alike.

The *aspirations* of the students and the community also shape the choices that teachers have. If the prevailing interest of the students (and indeed their parents and the entire community) is to get out of school and get a job, the teachers' choices are obviously constrained. Similarly, if the community expects all students to score above the eightieth percentile on every standardized test, that surely constrains the teacher's range of choices.

The Economic Context

Many researchers have concluded that social class, which is largely determined by wealth in the United States, is *the* substantial correlate of academic achievement. Studies show that students from rich families tend to do well in school. In families where education is valued, incomes tend to be higher because one or both parents will often be employed in professional or managerial positions that require substantial education. In poorer families where the parents are employed in hourly positions or where the major source of income is welfare, often little value is placed on education because advanced study is not felt to be related to economic survival.

Another factor complicating the economic context is student employment. In a survey done in the Denver, Colorado, area in 1985, 52 percent of the high school students had full-time or part-time jobs, and of that group 58 percent earned $100 or more per month while going to school full time. The fact that school is not a true full-time enterprise for so many students surely influences teaching practice.

However, the issue is even more complicated than the wealth and occupational patterns of families and students. Considerable unevenness exists in the funding of schooling from state to state, district to district, and even school to school. For example, in the Denver metropolitan area, comprising nine separate school districts, the general fund per-pupil expenditure varied from a low of $3,159 to a high of $4,446 in 1985. In the same districts, per-pupil costs devoted to teachers' salaries ranged from $2,462 to $3,687. In the San Antonio, Texas, metropolitan area, comprising twelve separate school districts, the general fund per-pupil expenditure varied from a low of $2,382 to a high of $4,073 in 1985. Per-pupil costs in the same districts devoted to teachers' salaries ranged from $874 to $1,811. One can see that even in a group of relatively similar school districts, the expenditures for education may vary substantially.

One has only to visit and compare the facilities in core-area schools in major cities with those outside the core to realize the unevenness of expenditures among school districts.

The Linguistic Dimension

The linguistic context involves the languages that students and the community speak. However, this context also takes dialects into consideration and the level of complexity of English as it is used in the school and in the wider community. Each constrains the teaching of English. The organic field model suggests that teachers of English must understand the linguistic contexts of their students and community and use that knowledge in making choices for teaching.

The number of bilingual programs offered in various states illustrates the magnitude of the problem caused by the diverse linguistic contexts in this country. In 1983, California had 113 separate programs designed to prepare teachers for bilingual classrooms. More than 575 programs were offered throughout the nation in that year. The language communities served range from Aleut in Alaska to Yiddish in New York. Clearly, the educational community is concerned about the linguistic context. However, little serious attention has been given to how this context specifically shapes the teaching of English. English teachers ignore this variable to the detriment of their students.

The dialects of the larger community and the student community also shape the teaching of English. English teachers are perennially concerned about whether instruction is best provided through the informality of the dialects spoken by students or through the more formal "standard" dialect. This conflict illustrates the importance of dialect as a determiner of classroom practice. The standard dialect is often made a matter of official policy in schools, with the policy being set by boards of education, administrators, departments, or individual teachers.

The level of student sophistication in English itself is also a matter of considerable importance to the classroom. It gets almost no official notice, even though it is a major context variable for the teacher. Students come to the English classroom with greatly varying levels of ability. Some come from homes where the spoken language is sophisticated and where complex English syntax and vocabulary are used; other students come from homes where only rudimentary, "survival" English is spoken. Some students who have read widely have a substantial, well-developed understanding of English; others have seldom read at all. The unevenness of students' linguistic sophistication is a major context variable for the teaching of English.

Policy

Policy is also an important context variable to the English teacher. All too often, the teacher is unaware of the constraining effect that policies have on instructional choices. However, the lack of awareness does not lessen the impact of the policy context.

The Human Dimension

This variable is most often represented in what boards of education and other elected officials say about educational policy and practice. The stated philosophy and goals of the board tend to be broad and meaningless. They are probably less important to the English teacher than the board's implicit philosophy, which is acted out in budgets, rules and regulations, and hiring practices.

The real constraints on teaching practice come from the policy-making body. Boards of education seem to share a common expectation that their students will score above average on standardized tests. That expectation hits English teachers hard, since it often requires them to emphasize a content matching that of the standardized tests being used in the district. The result is that many English teachers violate the substance portion of the organic field model in trying to implement what they perceive to be appropriate responses to policy. Today's aspirations of boards of education in many states and districts often relate strongly to test scores; tomorrow's aspirations may relate to football and marching bands, which have little influence on the English classroom.

The Legal Dimension

Laws are the most overt instruments of public policy. They constrain the behavior of teachers by limiting certain actions such as corporal punishment. Laws restrict discretionary behavior, as in reporting child abuse. They determine the makeup of classes, as in desegregation and mainstreaming. They routinely determine significant parts of the curriculum when they require that specific things be taught. Increasingly, laws are affecting the entire curriculum by requiring schools to submit to standardized testing programs. The interaction between legal requirements and fiscal policies is especially acute in states where funding is tied to performance on such required instruments.

The Fiscal Dimension

Increasingly, the context of education is being shaped by fiscal policies. Laws are enforced by withholding funds, for example, in desegregation and mainstreaming cases. Teachers are agreeing to take larger classes in return for salary increases. Textbook purchases are frequently delayed during times of fiscal tightness. Instructional equipment is especially susceptible to the shifting winds of fiscal policy.

Fiscal policies clearly establish a context for instruction and can be acutely felt in the English classroom. This effect is especially strong in relation to class size and materials available to the teacher.

The Physical Dimension

The physical context provided for instruction is a crucial variable in constraining what the English teacher does. For example, most schools are ill-suited for individualized instruction because of their architecture. Few provide adequate space for a real writing lab. Team-teaching opportunities are restricted in many buildings because the classrooms were built to a standard size.

The location of the school building is another physical contextual variable that constrains teaching. When educational opportunities outside the school seem appropriate to a lesson, the teacher may not always be able to take advantage of them. Human, legal, and fiscal constraints may also inhibit opportunities to extend class activities outside the school building.

Individually, the different policy variables seem highly restrictive. Collectively, they make classroom decisions extremely difficult. The interactions that can occur among all of these variables are legion.

The Profession

Teachers themselves bring many variables to the classroom. In fact, the richness of our best English departments may well be a result of the wide variation in the personal context of the members of those departments.

The Teacher

The teacher's philosophy, academic background, intellect, experience, personality, interests, and aspirations all shape what happens in the classroom. The fact that some teachers love literature probably means that they feel honor-bound to help their students develop that same love. Bright teachers may sometimes overestimate what their students can do, but will seldom be found wanting by gifted students who wish to go beyond the mean. Teachers of more average intellect may have to compensate through other devices. Those with wide experience of the world will always be at an advantage because they can draw parallels between what is being studied and the outside world. Teachers with high aspirations for their students may sometimes be disappointed, while those who expect little from their students may get little in return. However, the degree to which these variables influence teaching is often determined by outside factors.

The Department

Either directly or indirectly, the department plays a significant role in determining how and to what extent the personal attributes of teachers influence classroom activity. The department's *philosophy,* stated or unstated, places a limit on teaching strategy. The department's *breadth,* that is, the degree of difference among the faculty, also exerts pressure on individual teaching. The *depth* of the faculty, that is, the number of teachers trained in English and experienced in teaching it as opposed to the number of beginners and interlopers from other disciplines, makes a significant impact on what can and cannot be done in classrooms. The *procedures* through which a department conducts its business are important; how the faculty are involved, how classes are assigned, how texts are selected contribute to the sense of freedom that individuals have in conducting classes. If an authoritarian department chair makes all the decisions, the chances are good that relatively common classroom practices will predominate. If teachers freely participate in departmental policy-making, the chance for individual variation from the departmental norm is magnified.

Most of the variables outside an individual teacher's control may seem to limit, rather than enhance, the freedom to choose teaching strategies. That is typically the case. However, departmental policy can, on rare occasions, provide the stimulus for teachers to go beyond a rather narrow present state (say of academic background or experience) and expand certain personal attributes. Most district-level officials believe that to be the desired outcome of a centralized curriculum, for example. In many situations, however, much of what happens at the departmental and district levels is stultifying, not stimulating.

The Larger Profession

The larger profession is probably more effective than the department in stimulating teachers to seek new academic and experiential levels. Through introducing teachers to new theories, practices, and materials, the larger profession encourages teachers to develop and change. But it also limits their options by maintaining traditions. Further, as certain practices become popular, a "bandwagon" effect seems to move through the profession. Especially when the bandwagons start in disciplines other than English, the innovations may become more constraining than freeing.

Summary of the Context Portion

The context in which teachers operate is clearly an important variable in expanding or limiting the choices they make in the classroom. Teachers must consider the community in which they teach and also the student community they serve. The values and actions of their governing boards also influence their actions.

Teachers' personal attributes influence their options, along with the values, characteristics, and actions of colleagues in their department. State and district policies also influence their options, as do the values and actions of their colleagues in the larger profession.

All disciplines suffer from contextual restrictions. However, English presents a particularly difficult situation because of the amount of school time devoted to its study and its long tradition of being related to learning to read (and even speak). Context tends to constrain significantly the English teacher's opportunity to implement innovative curricular and teaching strategies.

Integrating Content and Context

Content and context are of course not isolated from each other. While scholars often analyze them separately, in practice they interact extensively in the English classroom. Both provide the framework within which the teacher must work. Together they constrain what the teacher can do.

Only when the substance, skills, and processes of English intersect do we have an accurate representation of the content of the discipline. By the same token, only when the community, policy, and profession variables intersect do we have a true reflection of the context in which English is taught. One might of course go even further and say that only when these two intersecting sets of variables come together do we have the reality of the English classroom. Figure 1 graphically illustrates the various points of intersection.

What then should English teachers do with the organic field model? Several possibilities exist:

1. Teachers should try to engage students in all three content areas in every class.

2. They should try to include each of the sub-areas of the content dimension in each unit of instruction.

3. They should be aware of the context variables that constrain the range of behaviors possible for them.

4. They should consider whether to accommodate to the context, attempt to change it, or violate it knowingly as they plan and

conduct instructional activities. The model expects all decisions to be purposeful and always based on the best knowledge available.

The Model

Can our discipline be as complex as the model suggests? Assuming that the model's twenty-nine variables represent the teaching of English, the researcher would be faced with an incredibly complex set of possible interactions (something like 2^{29}). Sadly, our discipline is probably even more complex than this. However, the intent of this report is to suggest that, unless we look broadly at English teaching from the perspective of both content and context, we will not provide many insights useful to the profession.

Consider the following illustration:

A Research-into-Practice Situation

Why does the study of grammar, mechanics, spelling, and vocabulary in isolation from the teaching of rhetoric and composition continue when both research and experience suggest that this approach is inappropriate?

Content Variables

1. *Substance.* The subcomponents of our discipline have not been integrated in practice except in rare situations. Our historical traditions emphasize separation over integration. Besides, compartmentalizing the subcomponents is easier than integrating them.
2. *Skills.* In spite of considerable research evidence to the contrary, it is commonly believed that teachers can teach skills out of context and expect students to apply them in context.
3. *Process.* The behaviorist assumption of parts-to-whole learning is applied inappropriately in this case. Writing involves a rather well-studied cognitive process. That process provides for learning mechanics in the context of their use, but never in isolation from the writing itself.

Context Variables

1. *Community.* The educational experiences of most parents, as well as of most students, have been in the isolated-skills tradition—and tradition dies hard. Also, reductionism is so common in schooling and even in society that students and parents alike believe that only parts-to-whole learning is truly worthwhile. Since the mechanical dimension of writing comprises "parts" at what seems to be a fundamental level, some people consider it logical to teach mechanics first.

2. *Policy.* Boards of education like standardized tests, which measure mechanics in isolation. It is natural to assume that, since the components are tested in isolation, they should be taught in isolation.
3. *Profession—Teacher.* Many teachers do not write much; as a result, they have little personal experience on which to base integrating the various skills into composition instruction. Teachers themselves are often products of a reductionist system and are regularly reassured that the parts-to-whole approach to teaching is best. Most teachers, too, do not like to read "all those themes" and prefer systems that simplify rather than complicate their lives. Teaching grammar and mechanics in isolation from writing may also reflect on the teacher's preparation to teach, since many teacher preparation programs give inadequate attention to the teaching of rhetoric and composition.
4. *Profession—Department.* Most department heads segment instruction by subdiscipline as they make teaching assignments. It is easier to label and teach a class in grammar and mechanics than a class called "English B," which has a poorly or ambiguously defined content.
5. *Profession—The larger profession.* Most state and district curricula are tied to the standardized tests adopted by their boards of education. As a result, it is an easy step to a reductionist curriculum dedicated to enhancing the results of these tests. Too little attention is given to translating the results of research into classroom practices and standardized tests. Further, grammar-as-an-end-in-itself texts that purport to teach composition are displayed at conventions, as if with the blessing of the National Council of Teachers of English.

The Student Teaching Experience: A Case Study

Only when the two major sets of variables—content and context—come together do we have the reality of the English classroom. What, then, would the application of the model reflect in the teaching of English? Let us take a short visit to a community called English Haven.

Ms. Horn, a student teacher, had turned twenty-four during the Thanksgiving holiday before the spring semester in which she was to student-teach in the English Haven Independent School District. In high school she had been a band member and a member of the National Honor Society. She was also active in church groups. Her love of English was apparent in her choice of an English composite major, which meant that not only would she major in English, but she would take other courses, such as journalism and speech, in support of English. The only drawback was that she could be certified to teach only English and might therefore find it somewhat difficult to gain a position.

Ms. Gabriel was the eleventh grade English teacher to whom Ms. Horn was assigned as a student teacher. Ms. Gabriel taught five classes:

three sections of regular junior English and two sections of what was called "trailer" junior English, that is, a class in which the students were taking the course again. Ms. Horn's experience would therefore give her the chance to work with students who were for one reason or another unsuccessful in the English classroom, as well as with students who were relatively successful.

Since the student teaching was to last an entire semester, Ms. Gabriel suggested that Ms. Horn observe in the classroom for the first week or two, and that she use a journal in which to record her observations and raise questions about the kinds of activities provided the students. When Ms. Horn asked what the students would be studying initially, she was told that throughout the semester they would have experiences that combined literature, language, and rhetoric, although a greater emphasis might be given to one or another of these areas during a unit. Skills would be developed within this content, using various processes to involve the students in the classroom activities. Ms. Gabriel then shared the following information with Ms. Horn about English Haven:

Context Variables

Ms. Gabriel has determined the following context variables:

I. Community: English Haven has a population of 55,000, not including the 20,000 students who attend the state-supported university in the town.
   A. *Social-psychological:* The schools in English Haven are fully integrated, with a student population mean IQ somewhat above 100. The parents want a good education for their children.
   B. *Economic:* The town has a mixture of white-collar and blue-collar workers. About 25 percent of the students hold part-time jobs. The parents are willing to pay taxes to have good schools.
   C. *Linguistic:* Although some Vietnamese have joined the community, ESL bilingual instruction seems necessary only in the lower grades.
II. Policy
   A. *Human:* School board members are from various walks of life, including professors, clergy, and blue-collar workers. The students get along well with each other and there is little trouble among ethnic groups. All students must meet the basic skills test requirement for graduation.
   B. *Legal:* The schools have closed campuses, and teachers are supported in classroom management and discipline through school board regulations.
   C. *Fiscal:* Money is provided for basic materials.

D.*Physical:* The school buildings are well-maintained, and the classroom desks are movable.

III. Profession

A.*Teachers:* Seventy-five percent of the teachers are white; 25 percent are black. All are certified, although 10 percent are teaching in fields with less than the preparation required by state law.

B. *Department:* The English department has a developed, standard curriculum. The teachers agree that students need to increase their reasoning skills.

C. *The larger profession:* Ninety percent of the English teachers belong to NCTE and are aware of practices such as student-centered activities.

Content Variables

Since the English department members agreed to give increasing emphasis to the development of reasoning skills, Ms. Gabriel shared with Ms. Horn the following unit of work she had developed to meet the reasoning skills objective:

I. Substance: Where does one find reasoning?

A.*Language:* In the relationship of thought to expression

B. *Literature:* In the expression of characters in literature

C. *Rhetoric:* In argumentation and persuasion

II. Processes: How does one learn to think?

A.*Affective:* In the use of a student's symbolic universe

B. *Cognitive:* In the activation of students' thinking

C. *Creative:* In allowing for student expression

III. Skills: What increases one's ability to think?

A.*Reading:* Literary embodiment of concepts

B. *Writing:* The activation of the composing process

C. *Listening:* The activation of listening episodes

D.*Speaking:* The activation of speaking episodes

To bring together the content and context variables, Ms. Gabriel titled her unit "The Inquiring Mind." The skills and concepts she incorporated into her unit include the following:

Language:	1. Thought and language shape each other.
	2. Language is symbolic.
Literature:	1. Connotation in literature is many times more significant than denotation.
	2. Drawing implications from literary selections is necessary to deal successfully with literature.

Rhetoric: 1. Argument is that form of discourse that attempts to win assent to a belief or opinion.
2. Deductive reasoning is one method of argumentation.
3. Persuasion is that form of discourse that presents arguments as motives for some proposed action.

To implement her unit, Ms. Gabriel designed the following activities:

1. The initiating activity will be class consideration of a Peanuts cartoon in which Lucy is reading a book. She closes it and walks away, stating, "I give up. There's no use trying. No matter how hard I try I can't read between the lines." The students will be asked to interpret Lucy's statement and the degree to which they associate with Lucy's feelings.

2. If reading is defined as a thinking process, the reader needs to have information and needs practice in activities such as (a) extracting and organizing meanings common to two or more statements, (b) supplying meanings not stated precisely, (c) speculating on what happened between events, (d) anticipating what will happen next, and (e) reasoning from cause to effect. The second activity will therefore be to read the first page only of the Shirley Jackson short story "After You, My Dear Alphonse." At this point in the story, Mrs. Wilson sees Boyd with his arms loaded with split kindling wood. The class will then be asked its impression of Mrs. Wilson. (In practice, the vast majority of students see Mrs. Wilson only as a typical mother.) The students will then finish reading the story, after which they will again be asked their impression of Mrs. Wilson. (In practice, the vast majority of students see her as prejudiced.)

3. Students will begin to work through Mrs. Wilson's thoughts (beliefs) and language:
   A. Mrs. Wilson turned to Johnny. "Johnny," she said, "what did you make Boyd do? What is that wood?" (slavery image)
   B. "There's plenty of food for you to have all you want."
   C. "Boyd will eat anything."

4. Students will then extend Mrs. Wilson's enthymemes into full categorical syllogisms:
   A. A member of a Negro family is not a person who has all the food he or she wants. Boyd is a member of a Negro family. Therefore, Boyd is not a person who has all the food he wants.
   B. Negroes are people who will eat anything. Boyd is a Negro. Therefore, Boyd is a person who will eat anything.

5. The students and teacher will work through the rules of deductive reasoning and categorical syllogisms.

6. The students will role-play extensions to the short story:
   A. Boyd goes home, and his mother asks him about the day's activities.
   B. Mrs. Wilson's neighbor calls, and Mrs. Wilson tells her about Boyd.

   The role playing is designed to evaluate student understanding of character development and story theme, and to provide speaking episodes.

7. Additional activities will include the use of pictures illustrating Boyd and Mrs. Wilson twenty years later. The students will improvise a conversation between the two. They will also listen to or read the lyrics from "You've Got to Be Taught to Hate and Fear" from the musical *South Pacific* and analyze the assumptions underlying the lyrics.

8. Copies of the Declaration of Independence will be distributed to the students for analysis with the context of the times (the Age of Reason). The teacher and students will work through the document, leading to an understanding that it is structured by the categorical syllogism expanded by points added to prove the major and minor premises (epichireme) and its blending of logic and rhetoric.

9. Using the overhead projector, the teacher will project only the caption for the Wind Song perfume ad, "I can't seem to forget you. Your Wind Song stays on my mind." Three pictures of men's faces will then be projected over the caption, one at a time. Two of the pictures will be of older men to contrast with the young, handsome man used in the actual ad. Students will select the picture they want for the caption and share their reasons for the choice. This activity should allow them to examine some possible faulty generalizations about people at differing stages of life. A general discussion of persuasion and persuasive techniques through visual and verbal expressions will ensue.

10. The Wind Song activity leads to a variety of student activities:
    A. Resolved: Advertising nowadays is too dishonest.
       Debate: To persuade an audience with a promise of joy or pleasure is to deal with them as selfish people. It suggests that the persuader does not respect them as reasonable, disciplined individuals who are capable of altruism.

B. The class will be divided into groups and given a product. Each group will devise strategies to persuade an audience to buy the product.
C. The students will select a speech by Martin Luther King, Jr., John F. Kennedy, or another famous speaker and will summarize it and describe the apparent purposes of the speaker.
D. The students will develop deductive arguments to prove such generalizations as the following:
Schools should be open twelve months each year.
Television is good for viewers.
E. The students will write critiques of editorials or letters to the editor.

11. In a culminating activity, the teacher will prepare various episodic passages from *To Kill a Mockingbird*. The students will use these passages to discuss how the episodes would be reported by different characters, and they will rewrite the passages from a different perspective. The criteria for evaluating the students' work will be the skills and concepts designed for this unit approach to the teaching of English. (*To Kill a Mockingbird* will have been read and discussed in an earlier unit.)

Ms. Gabriel will use the following references for the unit:

Educational Policies Commission. 1961. *The Central Purposes of American Education.* Washington, D.C.: National Education Association.

Glatthorn, A. A. 1980. *A Guide for Developing an English Curriculum for the Eighties.* Urbana, Ill.: National Council of Teachers of English.

Lazarus, A. L., and R. Knudson. 1967. *Selected Objectives for the English Language Arts, Grades 7–12.* Boston: Houghton Mifflin.

Loban, W., M. Ryan, and J. R. Squire. 1969. *Teaching Language and Literature, Grades 7–12,* 2d ed. New York: Harcourt, Brace and World.

Moffett, J., and B. J. Wagner. 1976. *Student Centered Language Arts and Reading, K–13: A Handbook for Teachers,* 2d ed. Boston: Houghton Mifflin.

The substance, processes, and skills of English have been designed to intersect in this unit, and the contextual framework of community, policy, and profession variables were considered in formulating the unit. The unit was thus prepared within the framework of the organic field model of the teaching of English.

While the student teacher was observing the implementation of Ms. Gabriel's unit, she drew several conclusions:

1. The students were given continual feedback.

2. Assessment of the students was based on several performances.

3. The students were given many examples and applications.

4. Classroom activities were very clear, and the teacher was enthusiastic about them. In addition, the teacher allowed for flexibility in her planning.

5. The teacher expected the students to do well.

6. A number of oral activities preceded writing activities.

7. The students searched for memories of their own that could be used in their writing activities.

8. Most importantly, English was seen holistically, not as a fragmented, nonunitary subject.

After the unit had been taught, Ms. Horn shared her conclusions with Ms. Gabriel and wondered if she would ever be able to do as well. Ms. Gabriel reassured Ms. Horn that she would guide her throughout the semester and would provide her with many sources that would help her understand and implement activities for the effective teaching of English.

Conclusion

A good model should be sensitive enough to permit one to criticize practice systematically. However, a good model should also allow another person to critique the critic's analysis point by point. The above example illustrates the robustness of this model.

A critic should be able to go through these critiques and, with the overall model as a background, agree or disagree point by point with the analyses. The model forces one to focus critiques on salient characteristics of the discipline and to detect weak points.

The organic field model appears to be robust enough to serve as a guide for the curriculum maker and the teacher; it can also provide a reference point for both research and criticism. The model should be especially useful to methods teachers, particularly when they decide to use observations and simulations. The model should provide a frame of reference that permits teachers to make informed decisions about what to do in the classroom rather than forcing them into artificial, generic behaviors that do not emerge from the true content and context of the English classroom.

II Research on Teaching: Presage Variables

William H. Peters
Department of Educational Curriculum and Instruction
Texas A&M University

Research on teacher effectiveness is aimed at finding out why some teachers are consistently more successful than others in maximizing student learning. As Medley (1977) states, "The teacher teaches, but the pupil learns." (70) Research results that specify which teaching variables affect learning are becoming increasingly dependable. It is therefore important that the results become known and incorporated into teacher preparation programs and into the classrooms of practicing teachers.

Toward Defining English Teacher Effectiveness

Concern about the competence of teachers has led to national interest in assessing competency. Medley (1982) distinguishes among teacher competency, competence, performance, and effectiveness in the following manner:

1. Teacher competency is defined as any single skill, area of knowledge, or professional value that a teacher possesses and that is believed to be relevant to successful teaching.

2. Teacher competence is defined in terms of repertoire; how competent a teacher is depends on his or her repertoire of competencies.

3. Teacher performance refers to what a teacher actually does on the job, rather than to what he or she can do. Performance is therefore specific to the job situation.

4. Teacher effectiveness refers to the effect that the teacher's performance has on pupils. (2–4)

Denemark and Nelli (1981) argue that in quality teacher education teaching is more than a synthesis of basic and pedagogical skills and familiarity with subject matter. Rather, teaching is a complex profession

25

necessarily viewed through a prism of knowing, doing, and being. This view, which is in keeping with that of national committees investigating teaching, is clearly reflected in *A Statement on the Preparation of Teachers of English and the Language Arts* (Larson et al. 1976). As stated in the introduction to its guidelines:

> Teachers must know their disciplines thoroughly and be able to employ their knowledge—to draw upon it or act upon it as needed—in planning work with, or activities for, their students. The following paragraphs deal first with the knowledge teachers need. But these paragraphs focus most of their attention on what the teacher drawing upon that knowledge must be able to do, and on the attitudes needed by a teacher in order to work effectively with the varied groups of students in today's schools.(5)

The Standing Committee on Teacher Preparation and Certification argues that language study should be approached holistically. The committee takes this position in *Guidelines for the Preparation of Teachers of English Language Arts* (Wolfe et al. 1986), a revision of Larson et al.'s 1976 statement. The revised document not only reaffirms the view of teaching as a complex profession, but clearly delineates the perhaps even more complex act of the *teaching of English* within the profession. As Smith (1983) asserts, the "teacher interacts with the student in and through the content, and the student interacts with the teacher in the same way." (491)

The concepts embedded in the guidelines are also striking in their similarities to the organic field model of the teaching of English (chapter 1 of this report), for the concepts refer to (1) English as a process; (2) the relationships among linguistic, cognitive, and affective processes; (3) the idea of context; and (4) the interrelatedness of speaking, listening, reading, and writing. The concepts also refer to the need for affective models of instruction; the interrelationships of reading/literature, composition, listening, speaking, and viewing; the creative uses of language; and a sensitivity to the impact that events in the world outside the school may have on teachers, their colleagues and students, and the English language arts curriculum.

All of these concepts selected from the guidelines suggest that the committee members intuitively recognized the need for a construct of English teaching that encompasses the multifaceted dimensions of the act of teaching English. Teacher effectiveness, then, depends upon a number of constantly changing variables within a structure that allows English teachers to assimilate changes in a manner that affects their choices.

The purpose of this chapter is to share relevant findings from teacher effectiveness research, particularly as it relates to the teacher as a professional variable. Within this variable, the personal, academic, and experiential factors embodied in the teacher have an effect on the teaching-learning process.

Research in teacher effectiveness involves an investigation of the classroom teaching process and frequently follows a model such as that suggested by Dunkin and Biddle (1974). The model consists of four classes of variables: presage, context, process, and product (Figure 1, next page). *Presage variables* involve teacher characteristics such as personality and abilities. *Context variables* involve characteristics of the environment such as the pupil population and school buildings. *Process variables* involve the actual activities of both teachers and pupils in interaction. *Product variables* involve changes that occur in pupils as a result of classroom activities. For the purpose of the present discussion, and in the interest of relating the Dunkin and Biddle model to the organic field model, we will focus on presage variables.

Presage Variables

The Dunkin and Biddle (1974) model was designed not only to aid understanding of the teaching process, but to enable a summary of research knowledge. Dunkin and Biddle consider knowledge of teaching to fall into six classes:

1. The conceptualization and study of teaching processes
2. The rate at which teaching processes occur in the typical classroom
3. The relationship between contexts and processes in teaching
4. The relationship between presage conditions and teaching processes
5. The relationships among processes occurring in the classroom
6. The relationships between the processes and the products of teaching

These six classes of knowledge are not, of course, independent of one another. They are, however, convenient classifications for summarizing knowledge concerning teaching. (48–50)

This chapter focuses on presage variables and knowledge about the relationship between presage conditions and teaching processes. Presage variables concern teacher characteristics examined for their effect on the teaching process. They include teacher formative experiences, teacher training experiences, and teacher properties.

Teacher Formative Experiences

Formative experiences are those that individuals have had before teacher training and that contribute to the individual's personality. The primary

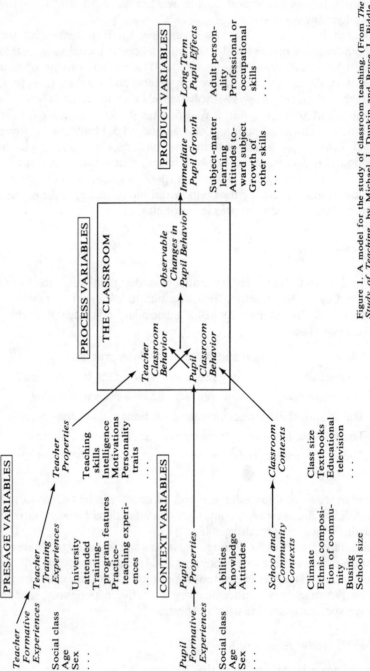

Figure 1. A model for the study of classroom teaching. (From *The Study of Teaching*, by Michael J. Dunkin and Bruce J. Biddle. Copyright © 1974 by Holt, Rinehart & Winston, Inc. Reprinted by permission of Holt, Rinehart & Winston, Inc.)

focus of early teacher effectiveness research was on the qualities of teachers who were effective in the classroom. A number of studies were directed toward the question of the effect that personal characteristics have on students. One of the most notable of these studies was conducted by Ryans (1960) for the American Council on Education. Its purpose was to describe teacher effectiveness and to compile information on the characteristics that define the teacher who produces a learning climate in the classroom. The study supported the theory that teacher characteristics do make a difference in the atmosphere and in the method of instruction and that "teacher behavior is determined in part by the teacher's personal and social characteristics (e.g., in the intellectual, emotional, temperamental, attitudinal, and interest domains) which have their sources in both the genetic (unlearned) and experiential (learned) backgrounds of the individual. Knowledge of such characteristics contributes to prediction, within limits, of teacher behavior." (370)

The study found that teachers with more successful patterns of classroom behavior tended to have strong interests in many areas, to prefer student-centered learning situations, to be independent, to have superior verbal intelligence, and to be willing to allow nondirective classroom procedures. Teachers with less successful behavior patterns tended to prefer teacher-directed learning situations, to value exactness, orderliness, and "practical" things, and to be less tolerant toward the expressed opinions of pupils. They were also more restrictive and critical in appraising the behavior and motives of other persons.

Ryans's study suggests that the teacher's personality, which is influenced by personal and social characteristics arising from the individual's genetic and experiential background, influences the learning climate in the classroom. These findings partly explain the shock that Squire (1969) felt when he learned that no more than 50 percent of the British teachers he observed had completed professional training in the teaching of English. According to Squire, the British teachers "seemed almost instinctively to possess a sure sense of classroom method" and to be "spontaneous, involved, and capable of eliciting genuine student response." (5) Since half of those teachers had had no professional training in the teaching of English, their success suggests that their methods, at least in part, were expressions of personality rather than training.

Ulin and Belsky (1971) point out that people who design programs for preparing secondary school teachers, as well as school administrators who hire graduates, assume that success both in studying the methods of teaching a discipline and in student teaching point to success in secondary school teaching. To test the predictive powers of selected variables, Ulin and Belsky used the University of Massachusetts program to train secondary school English teachers as a fairly representative program.

The criteria of success consisted of the grades that students received in their English methods course and in their student teaching. The data indicate that three variables, each used independently, can predict success in the methods course. The variables are (1) cumulative grade point average in all courses, (2) the grades received in required core English courses, and (3) the scores received on the verbal section of the Scholastic Aptitude Test.

When the three scores are combined with the average of a student's grades in elective English courses, the multiple equation in turn produces a slight rise in predictability. On the other hand, none of the selected variables, either independently or in any combination, predicts success in student teaching with any significant degree of reliability. The uniformly low predictive power of the academic variables used in student teaching suggests that if any significant correlates with success in practice teaching are to be uncovered, we are most likely to find them in the personality characteristics and nonacademic experience of prospective teachers.

It would be naive to assume that teacher trainers can completely change young adults who already possess personal and social characteristics arising from their genetic and experiential background. However, let us assume that research on teacher formative experiences (as related to presage variables) identifies certain teacher behaviors as desirable. The effectiveness of training programs might be enhanced by using the research findings to develop appropriate mechanisms to screen students for these programs. Alternatively, the findings might be used to provide experiences in the program to help all teachers work toward the identified desirable behaviors. Harvey (1970), who has studied beliefs and behaviors, suggests that it would be unrealistic to think of filling classrooms entirely with teachers who have an information-seeking and problem-solving orientation (Belief System IV), which he believes is needed in the classroom. He does suggest, however, that strong efforts should be made to impart some of the skills of System IV teachers to those who would be teachers.

Teacher Training Experiences

Teacher training experiences include the program features and student teaching provided in teacher preparation programs. In the more recent literature on teacher education, a predominant theme is that preparation programs should provide a pedagogical component emphasizing generic teaching competencies. For example, Howsam et al. (1976) used the term *professional culture* to designate the knowledge, skills, behaviors, attitudes, and values that make up the collective basis for practices and decision making by members of a profession. Another paper (Reynolds 1980) contains a substantive discussion of competency clusters that define a common core of requirements or a professional culture for all teachers. This paper evolved out of the Dean's Grants Projects, which were supported by the Bureau of Education for the Handicapped, U.S. Office of Education, for the purpose of redesigning teacher education to accord with the principles of Public Law 94–142. Lindsey (1978) described the generic competencies essential to teaching any curriculum to any age group in any setting. Denemark and Nutter (1980) proposed seven generic teaching competencies, not unlike those identified by Smith (1980). The revised *Guidelines for the Preparation of Teachers of English Language Arts* (1986) calls for teacher qualifications in knowledge, pedagogy, and attitudes.

Review of Research Related to Teacher Education[1]

During the past decade, significant advances have been made in identifying effective teaching behaviors, but probably very little of the research has found its way into teacher preparation programs. It is logical that the content of these programs embody the following areas supported by research efforts: effective teaching, language of the classroom, teacher planning and decision making, teaching context, effective schools research, and research on reading, writing, and mathematics learning (Koehler 1983). In addition, the processes and delivery systems used to provide this pedagogical content need to be developed, keeping in mind the various research evaluation findings of teacher preparation programs. The following material briefly reviews empirical evidence for effective teaching practices that candidates should integrate into their professional knowledge base.

Effective teaching. The often-cited works of Brophy and Evertson (1976a, 1976b), McDonald (1976), and Stallings (1976) exemplify process/ product findings, usually correlational, on the classroom behaviors and processes of effective teachers. These efforts were extended by the subsequent efforts of Evertson et al. (1983), Good and Grouws (1983), and others who used the correlational findings to establish training programs for teachers.

Efforts to determine the effects of these training programs based on research usually yielded positive results in terms of student achievement. Subsequently, lists of effective teaching practices began to appear in the literature of Good (1979) and Brophy (1983). Ironically, these teaching practices were very similar to the sequence of instructional moves (events

───────────────

1. This section is based on a review of research that was part of a proposal ("Using Research Knowledge to Improve Teacher Education") submitted by the Department of Educational Curriculum and Instruction, College of Education, Texas A&M University, and subsequently funded by the National Institute of Education, Washington, D.C. (1985).

of instruction) as presented by Gagné (1970, 1977). These instructional moves—gaining the attention of learners, providing objectives to learners, reviewing prerequisites, providing stimulus material with guidance, requiring learner performance of new learnings, providing feedback, assessing learning based on multiple performances, and providing multiple examples and applications for retention and transfer—have been verified by process/product research, as well as by research from instructional psychology (Gagné 1977; Klausmeier and Allen 1978; Glaser 1976).

The language of the classroom. Koehler (1983) states that sociolinguistic analyses of classroom language have identified a variety of communication problems between teachers and students who have different cultural heritages, ethnic backgrounds, and socioeconomic classes. Strickland (1983) suggests that one source of these communication problems is related to the controversy surrounding the language development of disadvantaged children. This controversy, described as the "deficiency versus difference issue," has often centered on the language of poor black children. Deutsch (1967) and Bereiter and Engelmann (1966) presented the "deficiency view" as a hypothesis to explain the poor reading achievement among many black children.

An alternative hypothesis, "the difference view," has been espoused by Baratz and Shuy (1969), Loban (1976), and Stewart (1965). According to this view, the language of poor black children is a nonstandard variety of English reflecting a formally structured linguistic system. Strickland (1983) notes that research in this field indicates that speakers of a nonstandard dialect incorporate standard English into their speech when teachers have positive attitudes about nonstandard dialects, have high expectations for children regardless of their speech patterns, understand students' oral language, and encourage the children to assess the appropriateness of different speech for different settings and purposes.

Planning and decision making. Since 1977, Clark and Yinger (1979) have examined the area of teacher planning. They concluded that teachers engage in up to eight types of planning: yearly, term, unit, weekly, daily, long-range, lesson, and short-range. The teachers who were studied identified unit planning as the most important type; only 7 percent of these teachers valued lesson planning as the most important.

Important considerations for planning appear to be drawn from student achievement and behavior records, with little systematic effort being exerted to weight data for diagnostic decisions (Shavelson and Stern 1981).

The unit of analysis for planning appears to center on classroom activities and their relation to the content of the lesson, rather than on the objectives of the lesson (Clark and Yinger 1979; Shavelson and Stern 1981; Zahorik 1975). Walberg and Waxman (1983) have provided an extensive research synthesis of instructional techniques and of learner and teacher characteristics that should influence planning decisions. For example, the researchers noted that all studies reviewed on the teaching traits of clarity, flexibility, and enthusiasm yielded positive results on the criterion variable under consideration. Griffin (1983) and Clark (1983) provide additional findings and discussion of research that can be applied to the instruction of planning.

Effective schools research. Research on school effects has signaled the need for school-based staff development programs that include the leadership of a strong principal, an orderly organizational climate, and high expectations for student achievement (Koehler 1983). Research on school effects dates back to the *Equality of Educational Opportunity Survey* (Coleman et al. 1966). This report indicated that variables contributing most of the variance in learner achievement were (in descending order) home environment, student body characteristics, teacher characteristics, and finally school facilities and curriculum. These findings produced a maelstrom of controversy about the limited significance that formal education has on learner achievement and other forms of student outcomes typically associated with the public schools. However, the report did stimulate public concern that focused directly on the effectiveness of teachers, curriculum, and schools in fostering learning.

Within the research community, subsequent analyses of the Coleman data provided additional findings; for example, teacher experience positively influences student achievement, and the race of the teacher influences cognitive verbal achievement (Hanushek 1972). An equally important consequence of these secondary analyses was the development of conceptual models for documenting the educational process. Typically, these models were constructed to explain an individual's educational achievement in terms of the following factors: individual and family characteristics, peer-group influences, genetic endowments, school resources, and study attitudes (Barro 1970; Hanushek 1972).

Subsequent work by Murnane (1975) and Denton, Kracht, and McNamara (1980) empirically documents the significant effects that classroom teachers have on achievement.

Reading, writing, and mathematics learning. Learning to write involves a number of transitions, for example, from oral to graphic expression. Vygotsky (1962) has suggested that this transition is a significant step in the development of symbolic thought. A second transition is from face-to-face communication to that with a remote audience, which is thought to be essential in the development of abstract logical reasoning. A third transition is from a language production system dependent at every level on inputs from a conversational partner to a system capable of autonomous operation (Bereiter and Scardamalia 1982).

Novice writing often appears to be egocentric, that is, the text is structured from the writer's point of view rather than from the frame of reference of the reader. Because of this phenomenon, it becomes difficult if not impossible to revise the material. Bereiter and Scardamalia (1982) have provided procedures to overcome this difficulty. Their work also addresses the use of strategies to conduct memory searches for greater text production and shifting from local to whole text planning.

One promising approach to narrative comprehension has been the development of schema theory, derived from Bartlett's (1932) work on adult memory of narratives. Bartlett's thinking has influenced current work on comprehension and text processing (Stein and Trabasso 1982). Schema theory is compatible with cognitive psychology's information-processing model of learning. Nevertheless, strategies for enabling learners to acquire the ability to read have tended to follow two rather divergent models, each of which espouses a link with the information-processing model. Labeled *holistic* and *subskill,* they are discussed by Strickland (1983), who briefly considered the implications that each approach has for preparing teachers.

Robert Davis (1983) presents an excellent discussion of contemporary research on diagnosis and evaluation in mathematics instruction, for example, error pattern analysis. Work in this area appears to be highly consistent with research in cognitive psychology, which explores the relationship between existing knowledge and the acquisition of new knowledge (Siegler and Klahr 1982).

Context of teaching. Context variables such as the subject being taught, grade level of the learner, type of curriculum design, and characteristics of the learner have substantial influence on instructional effects measured in terms of learner achievement (Koehler 1983). Walberg (1982), summarizing a decade of educational research, addresses a number of context issues such as the influence of open education on achievement, creativity, learner self-concept, attitude toward school, self-determination, independence, and freedom from anxiety. Ironically, achievement was the only dependent variable (learner characteristic) not overwhelmingly favored by open-concept schools (see Tables 4–7 in chapter 4). Further, Walberg (1982) cites extensive evidence on the relation of socio-psychological climate and learning and the influence of home environment on learner achievement. Other context variables associated with teaching-learning are treated in excellent papers by Edmonds (1983) and Soar and Soar (1983). These variables are also treated extensively in chapter 3 of this book.

Processes and delivery systems in teacher education. Over the past decade, inquiries at Texas A&M University have focused on teacher education programs as delivery systems. It seems appropriate to include these findings here not as sources of content for the program, but rather as suggestions for designing teacher preparation curricula:

1. Learners of student teachers who are education majors outperform their counterparts taught by noneducation student teachers (Denton and Norris 1981).

2. Average learner attainment is not influenced by the teaching field of the student teacher (Denton and Tooke 1981–82).

3. Supervisor ratings of teaching skills account for very little variation in cognitive attainment of learners of the student teacher (Denton and Norris 1980).

4. Planned instructional time by student teachers accounts for some variation in cognitive attainment among their learners (Denton and Norris 1980).

5. Approximately two-thirds of the objectives that a student teacher prescribed for a learner are mastered (Denton and Tooke 1981–82).

6. Approximately two-thirds of a student teacher's class will achieve a particular objective (Denton and Tooke 1981–82).

7. Cognitive performances by learners across instructional units planned and implemented by student teachers are relatively stable (Denton, Morris, and Tooke 1982).

8. Considerable variation in learner performance occurs across student teachers (Denton, Morris, and Tooke 1982).

9. Cognitive performance in subsequent courses on teaching methods is enhanced by completing a field experience early (Denton et al. 1982).

10. Attainment of higher-order objectives (analysis, synthesis) in subsequent courses on teaching methods is enhanced by completing a field experience early (Denton et al. 1982).

11. Morale ratings among teachers across all levels (kindergarten through secondary) during the semester of student teaching are very similar (Morris et al. 1980).

12. Morale during student teaching is not highly related to common concerns noted during student teaching (Morris et al. 1980).

13. Past academic performance (GPAs) of student teachers does not appear to influence cognitive attainment of their learners (Denton, Morris, and Tooke 1982).

Concluding Thoughts on Research on Teaching

Research on teaching and learning provides conclusive evidence that teachers *do* influence what happens to students in classrooms. Reviews cited on the context of the teaching-learning process indicate that effective teaching behaviors vary for students of different backgrounds and characteristics, as well as for different grade levels and subject areas. Teaching behaviors that have proved effective when used in moderation can prove equally ineffective if overused or applied under the wrong circumstances. These observations about the "conditionality" of research findings associated with teaching discourage the development of general rules of teaching.

Generalizations based on the research must also be guarded against because the effectiveness of various instructional techniques and teaching behaviors depends on the goals of instruction. Direct instruction and similar strategies that have successfully improved basic skills may not be as effective as other strategies if creativity, complex problem solving, or independent thinking become dependent variables. A fitting conclusion to this review comes from a Rand report by Wise et al. (1984):

> If markedly different teaching behaviors lead to divergent results that can be deemed equally desirable, one cannot identify a single, unidimensional construct called *effective teaching*, much less delimit its component parts. One can, at best, pursue alternative models of effective teaching, making explicit the goals underlying each.
>
> Clearly, the design of [teacher education] systems depends critically on educational goals; as conceptions of goals vary from unidimensional to multidimensional, so conceptions of appropriate teaching activities vary from easily prescribed to more complex teaching acts resting on the application of teacher judgment. In short, as one ascribes different degrees of generalizability to effective teaching behaviors and different weights to context-specific variables, one implicitly embodies different conceptions of teaching. The more complex and variable one considers the educational environment, the more one relies on teacher judgment to guide the activities of classroom life and the less one relies on generalized rules for teacher behavior. (10–11)

It is encouraging to note that teacher education institutions are beginning to incorporate into pre-service programs the social science research literature associated with teaching and learning and to validate frameworks being constructed for initial teacher preparation programs. It is imperative, however, that a model such as the organic field model of the teaching of English be employed as a prism through which research findings may be viewed for their applicability to the teaching of English.

Teacher Properties

Teacher properties consist of the measurable personality characteristics that the teacher takes into the teaching situation. The teacher's personality and teaching style, whether contrived or spontaneous, appear to influence the environment that the student responds and adjusts to. What transpires in the classroom between the teacher and student is apparently influenced to a great extent by the teacher. Alexander and Elson (1971) studied the effects that teacher-initiated interactions have on the achievements of students. Findings from this study emphasized the importance of affective teacher variables for student learning at higher levels. Harris (1973) found that the students of a teacher who was flexible, divergent, or creative increased their own creative behavior more so than did students of teachers who did not provide such modeling.

Experimental studies of questioning by Ward and Tikunoff (1975) and by the Stanford Program on Teaching Effectiveness (1976) found that students in classes where many recall questions were asked did slightly better on recall tests. Yet students did equally well on integrative questions regardless of what percentage of recall questions were asked in class. In a similar vein, Wright and Nuthall (1970) found significant positive results in student responses when teachers exhibited a probing behavior. Yet Brophy and Evertson (1976a) did not find a relationship between seeking improved responses and achievement. Other studies have involved areas such as direct and indirect instruction (for example, Flanders 1970; Samph 1974), teacher praise (for example, Soar 1973; Brophy and Evertson 1974; Stallings and Kaskowitz 1975), and teacher enthusiasm (for example, Mastin 1963; Brophy and Evertson 1976a).

To investigate the effects of teacher characteristics on pupil achievement, observing actual instruction in the classroom becomes paramount. Techniques for measuring classroom behaviors became available when Medley and Mitzel (1958) published the Observation Schedule and Record (OScAR) and when Flanders (1960) published the initial findings of his Interaction Analysis Categories system (FIAC). Rosenshine (1976) reported that the work of Flanders, Medley, Mitzel, and others ushered in the modern era of studies on teacher effectiveness. Even in this "modern era," however, relatively few studies that investigate the relationship between classroom instruction and student achievement have been conducted. The number of researchers involved is equally small.

Squire (1964), in his studies of adolescents' responses to short stories, emphasizes the teacher's role in the inquiry process. His work has led us to believe that after completing a reading, students have several responses to the text. All of the responses occur simultaneously and are related to

personal dispositions, thus indicating the complexity and highly individualistic nature of response patterns. If the teacher tolerates many opinions
and value scales, he or she may suggest ideas not previously thought of
or may foster discussion of initial ideas through enlargement and
modification.

The literature seems to support the assumption that teacher characteristics do have a significant effect on students. If learning outcomes
relate to teacher characteristics, then probably a teacher's tolerance of
ambiguity and preference for complexity would relate to a student's
openness to interpreting literature. Peters and Blues (1978) focused on
the effect that preference for complexity and tolerance of ambiguity, as
measured by the Co scale of the Omnibus Personality Inventory (OPI),
have on student achievement related to literature. The study suggested
that high Co OPI teachers contribute more positively than low Co OPI
teachers to students' written ability to interpret literature. The authors
noted the need for further classroom observation of the characteristics
attributed to high and to low Co scorers in order to define behaviors that
could be associated with effective and noneffective teachers.

If learning outcomes relate to high-complexity teachers, then it seemed
probable that a trait such as tolerance of ambiguity and preference for
complexity, as measured by the Co scale, would relate to cognitive verbal
reactions that the teacher creates in the classroom. A second study by
Peters and Amburgey (1982) focused on the differences between the
cognitive verbal reactions in the classrooms of high Co teachers and low
Co teachers. This study provided evidence that high-complexity teachers
move their students into higher levels of cognition, which encourages
student thinking. Pupils in both the high- and the low-complexity
classrooms were receiving basic information early in the semester. By
mid-semester, pupils in the low-complexity classrooms continued receiving basic information, while those in the high-complexity classrooms
moved on to other, more complex cognitive levels.

Travers's (1984) recent review of research on the teaching of poetry in
the classroom suggests that the particular teacher has more influence on
results than the particular method that the teacher uses. Particular
teachers appear to influence their pupils' attitudes even within the other
powerful influences of home, individual pupil personality, or the form of
poetry under study. The reviewer recommends ethnographical studies as
the research methodology for gaining increased understanding of the
complexities in teaching poetry. Evidence seems to suggest that it would
be worthwhile for teacher training institutions to develop ways of training
potential teachers in the behaviors that lead to successful teaching.

Conclusion: Presage Variables and Teacher Effectiveness

The review of teacher effectiveness research related to presage variables supports the view expressed by Koehler (1983) that effective teaching research should be part of the essential knowledge base of clinical supervision and cooperating teachers who assist students through their student teaching. The concluding section of the 1986 *Guidelines for the Preparation of Teachers of English Language Arts,* too, stresses the need for models of good teaching, the analysis of good teaching, and the observation of good teaching for prospective teachers of English language arts. If supervision in English education is to help improve instruction, Henry (1986) believes that some theory of instruction for English education must be found. The paradox, he contends, is that "English education is composed of an 'English' never sure of the nature of its substance, and an 'education' uncertain of the soundness of the kind of science it believes English teaching needs." (32) Perhaps in the wedding of those findings from effective teaching research within the organic field model of the teaching of English a beginning can be made.

References

Alexander, L., B. Elsom, R. Means, and G. Means. 1971. Achievement as a Function of Teacher-Initiated Student-Teacher Personal Interactions. *Psychological Reports* 28:431–34.

Baratz, J., and R. W. Shuy, eds. 1969. *Teaching Black Children to Read.* Urban Language Series, No. 4. Washington, D.C.: Center for Applied Linguistics.

Barro, S. M. 1970. An Approach to Developing Accountability Measures for the Public Schools. *Phi Delta Kappan* 52:196–205.

Bereiter, C., and S. Engelmann. 1966. *Teaching Disadvantaged Children in the Preschool.* Englewood Cliffs, N.J.: Prentice-Hall.

Bereiter, C., and M. Scardamalia. 1982. From Conversation to Composition: The Role of Instruction in a Developmental Process. In *Advances in Instructional Psychology,* Vol. 2, ed. R. Glaser, 1–64. Hillsdale, N.J.: Erlbaum.

Brophy, J. E. 1983. Classroom Organization and Management. In *Essential Knowledge for Beginning Educators,* ed. D. C. Smith, 23–37. Washington, D.C.: American Association of Colleges for Teacher Education. ED 237 455.

Brophy, J. E., and C. M. Evertson. 1974. Process-Product Correlations. In *The Texas Teacher Effectiveness Study: Final Report,* no. 74–4. Austin: Univ. of Texas at Austin, Research and Development Center for Teacher Education. ED 091 394.

————. 1976a. Context Effects on Classroom Process Variables, Report no. 76–10. Austin: Univ. of Texas at Austin, Research and Development Center for Teacher Education.

————. 1976b. *Learning from Teaching: A Developmental Perspective*. Boston: Allyn and Bacon.

Clark, C. M. 1983. Research on Teacher Planning: An Inventory of the Knowledge Base. In *Essential Knowledge for Beginning Educators*, ed. D. C. Smith, 5–15. Washington, D.C.: American Association of Colleges for Teacher Education.

Clark, C. M., and R. J. Yinger. 1979. *Three Studies of Teacher Planning*, Research Series no. 55. East Lansing: Michigan State Univ. ED 175 855.

Clark, C. M., et al. 1976. A Factorially Designed Experiment on Teacher Structuring, Soliciting, and Reaction. Research and Development Memorandum no. 147. Stanford: Stanford Center for Research and Development in Teaching. ED 134 591.

Coleman, J. S., E. Q. Campbell, C. J. Hobson, J. McPartland, A. M. Mood, F. Weinfield, and R. L. York. 1966. *Equality of Educational Opportunity*. Washington, D.C.: U.S. Government Printing Office.

Davis, R. B. 1983. Diagnosis and Evaluation in Mathematics Education. In *Essential Knowledge for Beginning Educators*, ed. D. C. Smith, 101–11. Washington, D.C.: American Association of Colleges for Teacher Education.

Denemark, G. W., and E. Nelli. 1981. Quality Teacher Education: A Context for Competency Assessment. In *Competency Assessment in Teacher Education: Making It Work*, ed. S. G. Boardman and M. J. Butler, 1–17. Washington, D.C.: AACTE and ERIC Clearinghouse on Teacher Education. ED 206 570.

Denemark, G. W., and N. Nutter. 1980. *The Case for Extended Programs of Initial Teacher Preparation*. Washington, D.C.: ERIC Clearinghouse on Teacher Education. ED 180 995.

Denton, J. J., and S. A. Norris. 1980. *Cognitive Attainment of Learners of Student Teachers: A Criterion for Attaining Accountable Teacher Preparation Programs*. College Station: Texas A&M University. ED 178 516.

————. 1981. Learner Cognitive Attainment: A Basis for Establishing a Student Teacher's Competence. *Texas Tech Journal of Education* 8:45–57.

Denton, J. J., J. B. Kracht, and J. F. McNamara. 1980. An Evaluation Design to Examine the Instructional Effects of Classroom Teachers. *Educational Evaluation and Policy Analysis* 2 (5): 5–15.

Denton, J. J., and D. J. Tooke. 1981–82. Examining Learner Cognitive Attainment as a Basis for Assessing Student Teachers. *Action in Teacher Education* 3:39–45.

Denton, J. J., J. E. Morris, and D. J. Tooke. 1982. The Influence of Academic Characteristics of Student Teachers on the Cognitive Attainment of Learners. *Educational and Psychological Research* 2:15–29.

Deutsch, M., et al. 1967. *The Disadvantaged Child*. New York: Basic Books.

Dunkin, M. J., and B. J. Biddle. 1974. *The Study of Teaching*. New York: Holt, Rinehart and Winston.

Edmonds, R. R. 1983. The Context of Teaching and Learning: School Effects and Teacher Effects. In *Essential Knowledge for Beginning Educators*, ed. D. C. Smith, 76–79. Washington, D.C.: American Association of Colleges for Teacher Education.

Evertson, C., E. Emmer, J. Sanford, and B. Clements. 1983. Improving Classroom Management: An Experiment in Elementary Classrooms. *Elementary School Journal* 84:173–88.

Flanders, N. A. 1960. *Teacher Influence, Pupil Attitudes, and Achievement: Final Report,* Project no. 397, U.S. Office of Education. Ann Arbor: Univ. of Michigan.

————. 1970. *Analyzing Teacher Behavior.* Reading, Mass.: Addison Wesley.

Gagné, R. M. 1970. *The Conditions of Learning.* 2d ed. New York: Holt, Rinehart and Winston.

————. 1977. *The Conditions of Learning.* 3d ed. New York: Holt, Rinehart and Winston.

Glaser, R. 1976. Components of a Psychology of Instruction: Toward a Science of Design. *Review of Educational Research* 46:1–24.

Good, T. L. March–April 1979. Teacher Effectiveness in the Elementary School: What We Know about It Now. *Journal of Teacher Education* 30 (2): 52–64.

Good, T. L., D. Grouws, and H. Ebmeier. 1983. *Active Mathematics Teaching.* New York: Longman.

Griffin, G. A. 1983. The Dilemma of Determining Essential Planning and Decision-making Skills for Beginning Educators. In *Essential Knowledge for Beginning Educators,* ed. D. C. Smith, 16–22. Washington, D.C.: American Association of Colleges for Teacher Education.

Hanushek, E. A. 1972. *Education and Race.* Lexington, Mass.: D. C. Heath & Co.

Harris, M. B. August 1973. Modeling and Flexible Problem-Solving. Paper presented at the annual convention of the American Psychological Association, Montreal. ED 085 111.

Harvey, O. J. 1970. Beliefs and Behavior: Some Implications for Education. *The Science Teacher* 37 (9): 11–12.

Henry, G. H. 1986. What is the Nature of English Education? *English Education* 18:4–41.

Howsam, R. B., D. C. Corrigan, G. W. Denemark, and R. J. Nash. 1976. *Educating a Profession: Report of the Bicentennial Commission on Education.* Washington, D.C.: American Association of Colleges for Teacher Education.

Klausmeier, H. J., and P. S. Allen. 1978. *Cognitive Development of Children and Youth: A Longitudinal Study.* New York: Academic Press.

Koehler, V. 1983. Introduction: A Research Base for the Content of Teacher Education. In *Essential Knowledge for Beginning Educators,* ed. D. C. Smith, 1–4. Washington, D.C.: American Association of Colleges for Teacher Education.

Larson, R., et al. 1976. *A Statement on the Preparation of Teachers of English and the Language Arts.* Urbana, Ill.: National Council of Teachers of English.

Lindsey, M. July–August 1978. Teacher Education: Reflections. *Journal of Teacher Education* 29:5–9.

Loban, W. 1979. *Language Development: Kindergarten through Grade Twelve.* Research Report no. 18. Urbana, Ill.: National Council of Teachers of English.

Mastin, V.E. 1963. Teacher Enthusiasm. *Journal of Educational Research* 56:385–86.

McDonald, F. J. Spring 1976. Report on Phase II of the Beginning Teacher Evaluation Study. *Journal of Teacher Education* 27:39–42.

Medley, D. M. 1977. *Teacher Competence and Teacher Effectiveness*. Prepared for the AACTE Committee on Performance-based Teacher Education.

————. 1982. *Teacher Competency Testing and the Teacher Educator*. Bureau of Educational Research, School of Education, 2–4. Reston: Univ. of Virginia.

Medley, D. M., and H. E. Mitzel. 1958. A Technique for Measuring Classroom Behavior. *Journal of Educational Psychology* 49:86–92.

Morris, J. E., B. S. Chissom, A. Seaman, and D. J. Tooke. 1980. Student Teacher Morale: A Comparison of Morale among Four Groups of Student Teachers. *The College Student Journal* 14:347–55.

Murnane, R. J. 1975. *The Impact of School Resources on the Learning of Inner City Children*. Cambridge, Mass.: Ballinger Publishing Co.

Peters, W. H., and B. S. Amburgey. 1982. Teacher Intellectual Disposition and Cognitive Classroom Verbal Reactions. *Journal of Educational Research* 76:94–99.

Peters, W. H., and A. G. Blues. 1978. Teacher Intellectual Disposition as It Relates to Student Openness in Written Response to Literature. *Research in the Teaching of English* 12:127–36.

Reynolds, M. C. 1980. *A Common Body of Practice for Teachers: The Challenge of Public Law 94-142 to Teacher Education*. Washington, D.C.: The American Association of Colleges for Teacher Education.

Rosenshine, B. V. 1976. Recent Research on Teaching Behaviors and Student Achievement. *Journal of Teacher Education* 27:61–64.

Ryans, D. G. 1960. *Characteristics of Teachers, Their Description, Comparison, and Appraisal: A Research Study*. Washington, D.C.: American Council on Education.

Samph, T. 1974. Teacher Behavior and the Reading Performance of Below-Average Achievers. *Journal of Educational Research* 67:268–70.

Shavelson, R. J., and P. Stern. 1981. Research on Teachers' Pedagogical Thoughts, Judgments, Decisions, and Behavior. *Review of Educational Research* 51:455–98.

Siegler, R. S., and D. Klahr. 1982. When Do Children Learn? The Relationship between Existing Knowledge and the Acquisition of New Knowledge. In *Advances in Instructional Psychology*, Vol. 2, ed. R. Glaser, 121–211. Hillsdale, N.J.: Erlbaum.

Smith, B. O. 1980. Pedagogical Education: How about Reform? *Phi Delta Kappan* 62:87–91.

————. 1983. Some Comments on Educational Research in the Twentieth Century. *Elementary School Journal* 83:488–92.

Smith, B. O., S. H. Silverman, J. M. Borg, and B. V. Fry. 1981. *A Design for a School of Pedagogy*, Report No. E-80-42000. Washington, D.C.: U.S. Department of Education.

Soar, R. S. 1973. *Follow Through Classroom Process Measurement and Pupil Growth, 1970-71 (Final Report)*. Gainesville: Univ. of Florida. ED 106 297.

Soar, R. S., and R. M. Soar. 1983. Context Effects in the Teaching-Learning Process. In *Essential Knowledge for Beginning Educators,* ed. D. C. Smith, 65–75. Washington, D.C.: American Association of Colleges for Teacher Education.

Squire, J. R. 1964. *The Responses of Adolescents while Reading Four Short Stories.* Research Report no. 2. Urbana, Ill.: National Council of Teachers of English.

————. 1969. The New Responsibilities of English Education. *English Education* 1:5–17.

Stallings, J. A. 1976. How Instructional Processes Relate to Child Outcomes in a National Study of Follow Through. *Journal of Teacher Education* 29:43–47.

Stallings, J. A., and D. H. Kaskowitz. April 1975. *A Study of Follow Through Implementation.* Paper presented at the annual meeting of the American Educational Research Association.

Stein, N. L., and T. Trabasso. 1982. What's in a Story: An Approach to Comprehension and Instruction. In *Advances in Instructional Psychology,* Vol. 2, ed. R. Glaser, 213–67. Hillsdale, N.J.: Erlbaum.

Stewart, W. 1965. Urban Negro Speech: Sociolinguistic Factors Affecting English Teaching. In *Social Dialects and Language Learning,* ed. R. W. Shuy. Urbana, Ill.: National Council of Teachers of English.

Strickland, D. S. 1983. The Development of Language and Literacy: Essential Knowledge for Effective Teaching and Learning. In *Essential Knowledge for Beginning Educators,* ed. D. C. Smith, 112–23. Washington, D.C.: American Association of Colleges for Teacher Education.

Travers, D. M. 1984. The Poetry Teacher: Behavior and Attitudes. *Research in the Teaching of English* 18:367–84.

Ulin, R. O., and T. B. Belsky. 1971. Screening Prospective English Teachers: Criteria for Admission to Teacher Education Programs. *Research in the Teaching of English* 5:165–78.

Walberg, H. J. Spring 1982. What Makes Schooling Effective? A Synthesis and Critique of Three National Studies. *Contemporary Education Review* 1:1–34.

Walberg, H. J., and H. C. Waxman. 1983. Teaching, Learning and the Management of Instruction. In *Essential Knowledge for Beginning Educators,* ed. D. C. Smith, 38–54. Washington, D.C.: American Association of Colleges for Teacher Education.

Ward, B. A., and W. J. Tikunoff. 1975. *Application of Research to Teaching.* Teacher Education Division Publication Series. Report no. A75-2. San Francisco: Far West Laboratory for Educational Research. ED 128 337.

Wise, A. E., L. Darling-Hammond, M. W. McLaughlin, and H. T. Bernstein. 1984. *Teacher Evaluation: A Study of Effective Practices.* Santa Monica, Calif.: Rand Corporation. ED 246 559.

Wolfe, D. T., et al. 1986. *Guidelines for the Preparation of Teachers of English Language Arts.* Urbana, Ill.: National Council of Teachers of English.

Wright, C. J., and G. Nuthall. 1970. Relationships between Teacher Behaviors and Pupil Achievement in Three Experimental Elementary Science Lessons. *American Educational Research Journal* 7:477–91.

Zahorik, J. A. 1975. Teachers' Planning Models. *Educational Leadership* 33:134–39.

III The Context Variable of the Organic Field Model: Research and Practice

Louise Grindstaff
Department of Secondary Education
California State University, Northridge

Historically, context variables and their relationship to teaching effectiveness have not been selected for research as often as other variables. Nevertheless, the recent research on school and teaching effectiveness may spur major interest in this area. Eventually the research could lead to major changes in educational policy and practice in English education as well as in the broader field of education.

Background

In this report, *context* as related to the organic field model will be defined as those variables that "concern the conditions to which the teacher must adjust—characteristics of the environment about which teachers, school administrators, and teacher educators can do very little" (Dunkin and Biddle 1974, 41). Teachers cannot easily control the effects of socioeconomic forces on students or of culturally entrenched biases about gender and ethnicity. Negative community attitudes towards schooling are difficult to counteract. Yet they invariably affect the school climate and interact with administrative policies.

Although teachers must adjust to the physical properties of the school plant, empirical research tells us little about the impact of these properties on teaching effectiveness. Even grade level and subject area assignments influence teaching effectiveness, but policymakers and administrators sometimes casually reassign teachers to another grade level or subject without allowing time for preparation. The effects of heterogeneity versus homogeneity in classes may also create more problems for the teacher than heretofore realized. An additional factor affecting teacher effectiveness is class size, which can make a crucial difference in English programs. And surely the nineteenth century architects of the traditional classroom could not have been divinely inspired when they designed the forty-seat classroom. Yet many of these classrooms throughout the United States are nearly full, regardless of the students' ages or the subject area. Also related to context are the effects that text materials and curriculum design have on teacher effectiveness.

In this discussion of research, context will be looked at from three points of view: community, policy, and the profession. Following this discussion, the actual context surrounding a beginning English teacher from a large urban school district will be briefly described.

Context and the English Classroom

The three content variables, namely, substance, skills, and process, found in the organic field model of teaching English are reasonably familiar to English and English language arts teachers. Aspects of the traditional tripod of literature, language, and composition seem to be recognizable even though the two sets of concepts are not actually the same. For example, in a lesson on composition, the rhetorical principle of "audience" might be classified as substance. This concept would probably be illustrated for the students by using examples of discourse (literature) for varying audiences. The process aspect of the model (prewriting, drafting, revising, editing, postwriting) would involve the cognitive, creative, and affective processes in creating a product, in this case a composition slanted to a specific audience. Aspects of instruction in composition would also involve attention to skills, either by practice, instruction, or remediation in reading, speaking, listening, and writing.

Thus the content variables are not seen as discrete, but rather as interrelated and organic, with many possible combinations. In contrast, the traditional model of language, literature, and composition assumes that each aspect is separate and discrete. An illustration of this is the common practice of teaching separate classes of grammar, composition, and literature from elementary school through college in the United States.

The context variables of the organic field model, although their effects are felt strongly and are often the subject of complaints and discomfort, have not been studied as often as the content variables. A basic assumption of the organic field model is that the variables must be in balance and interrelated if English instruction in the developmental grades is to be effective (see Figure 1, p. 6). For purposes of this discussion, the developmental grades include elementary and secondary schools. Therefore, when English instruction involves one variable to the exclusion of the others, the balance is destroyed, and in essence no English is taught. The lack of balance in actual classroom practice probably explains why recent curricular experiments with English, such as elective English, the back-to-basics movement, or the emphasis on process models of composition instruction, have ended in failure. The response model of teaching literature probably fell by the wayside for the same reason. We have also had periods where context—community concerns and relevance—may have overshadowed the content recognizable as English in the classroom.

In some schools, contextual concerns can overwhelm the efforts of teachers who may be focusing on matters related to content while ignoring the powerful force of context. One has only to try once to teach *Julius Caesar* to a class of tenth grade, inner-city students on a blistering Friday afternoon in southern California to understand the pervasive influence of context. As one exasperated teacher commented, "The only saving grace is that half of the students were at the beach and the other half were asleep. I think I was talking to myself."

Even teachers who try to integrate the content variables may have problems if they ignore the context variables. A tenth grade English teacher may focus the lesson on the power that a central image—such as the tree in John Knowles's *A Separate Peace*—has in controlling the events in a novel. The lesson may center on the study of literature (substance) and proceed through discussion and writing (skills) involving reflection, response, and text analysis (process). The subject of the novel seems appropriate enough for a tenth grade class. Yet there may be students for whom the teacher would have to construct elaborate "bridges" to maximize the possibility of an appropriate literary transaction necessary to successful instruction. For example, inner-city students may not accept the world of private school boys in the 1940s during a war that the students of the 1980s know only from their grandparents.

Educational Research and Methodological Problems

Common sense seems to dictate that the context would have great impact on what happens in an English classroom. Nevertheless there is a dearth of hard data to bolster the attempts of the English teaching profession to influence policy regarding context. The reason may very well lie in the methodologies that educational and other social scientists use to do research. Context is the most elusive variable to study and the most impossible to control with the usual methods. Hillocks (1984) points out the problem of researching the teaching of English through strictly empirical techniques. Currently, social scientists are disenchanted with empirical research; a study of teaching, using the artifice of controls and carefully identified variables and effects, may be fool's gold after all— easily seen, but not worth much.

Bolster (1983) suggests that theory courses in schools of education and other social sciences do not impress working teachers because theory and

practice refer to completely separate realities. He postulates that researchers (theorists) and working teachers perceive teaching quite differently
and also determine or verify it differently. Teachers work in classrooms
where "situation decisions" are made continuously throughout the day.
They may not have time to analyze and reflect on the data. Researchers,
on the other hand, are writing to researchers and not necessarily to the
teachers in the field.

Bolster reminds us that researchers are striving for recognition from
their peers and superiors. In fact, they may not necessarily be trying to
improve the profession of teaching. The primary goal of the teacher is to
find something that works well with a particular group of students within
a context. The researcher, however, is looking for a general principle that
applies in all situations. Valuing control, reliability, and observable
events, researchers will ignore or filter out the effects of unanticipated
contingencies such as heavy rains, flu epidemics, or winning an important
game. Researchers focus on small parts and are therefore reductionist in
their thinking. Teachers focus on whole classes functioning within school
environments and are inclusive in their attempts to manage the many
decisions necessary to successful teaching. Basically, teachers see teaching
as a process, something that is done in the classroom with people and
situations; researchers see teaching as an achievement resulting in a
product, usually a test score.

Bolster's essay underscores the need for a more useful approach to
the study of teaching. King (1978) suggested that writing be studied from
the context perspective, using ethnographic methods and focusing on
children's writing, teacher intervention, modes, and the specific factors
that influence writing, namely, events and environments. Herrington
(1985) completed an ethnographic study that carefully describes the
contexts for writing in two college chemical engineering courses.

In his meta-analysis of experimental treatment studies in composition,
Hillocks (1984) identifies the most powerful teaching mode in the studies
as the "environmental" mode. This mode is basically a combination of
teacher presentation and student group interaction on a writing problem,
with student involvement in writing processes. The environmental mode
appears to correspond to the effective teaching conditions described in
the organic field model. Hillocks makes the further point that, even with
the admitted limitations of empirical research, much can be learned from
the experimental effects of the past twenty years. Although we may not
see the whole truth, we can catch glimpses of possibilities for improvement, both in what we know about teaching and in the methodology of
research to increase our knowledge and effectiveness.

Purves (1984) argues for a combination of efforts from both the social
sciences and the humanities for looking at language education from its

many perspectives. Mishler (1979) suggests in his provocative essay on context that the usual scientific approach to studying education may be impossible. We cannot produce laws and principles that are context-free, nor can we isolate the effects of context from other variables, for the context may alter the action, the actor, and the observer. Mishler therefore suggests that educational researchers use the techniques of sociolinguistics and ethnomethodology. Certainly, English educators in university, school district, or state department settings must focus their energy on improving the effectiveness of the English teacher in the classroom. It seems reasonable to use the findings of both empirical and ethnographic research to that end and to work towards the development of improved research methodologies.

The Need for Unification in English Education

Previous attempts to describe what we do in English education have focused too narrowly on one variable, often in isolation. We recognize that this focus and separation may be necessary in advanced English study at university levels. But when it comes to the lower levels, this approach does not seem to work. Our recent experience with Project English seemed to prove that curricula consisting primarily of substance does not succeed in the lower grades.

We have also tried teaching the various aspects of our subject as separate skill strands, as in spelling on Monday, literature on Tuesday, vocabulary on Wednesday, composition on Thursday, and tests on Friday. Teachers thus found themselves teaching separate subjects on different days, and often separate subjects within a given class period. The resultant confusion further increased the distance between what the leadership in NCTE and other English organizations describe as English and what often was happening in the classrooms. Even the common reaction of citizens to English teaching has more to do with grammar and spelling than with other aspects of English. Through state and district curriculum studies and reports, we have tried to unify English and to discourage the presentation of English as particles of skills, but the practice still persists in many English classrooms.

Research in Teacher Effectiveness

Many of the studies reviewed in this discussion do not focus on the subject of English as taught in the secondary school. Most deal primarily with reading and mathematics as taught in elementary schools. However, the influence of context on teaching effectiveness, even if studied in the larger framework, involves English instruction most intimately, since all students study English in all grades of elementary and secondary schools.

The context of an English classroom varies according to time, population, place, political happenings, and state of mind of the students, both collectively and individually. Each classroom is a distinct social unit with its own energy, and it is capable of assuming various shapes in response to events. The teacher's job is to work effectively with that class unit in the joint exploration of English.

The Context of Community

Although teachers may have been educated in the finest training programs possible for the teaching of English language arts, they will inevitably encounter the elusive and sometimes unknown variable of the pupils themselves. Some teachers become discouraged because the students are not the ideal learners they imagined in their university classes. Teachers of course have to teach in the real world of children from all backgrounds. The research reviewed in this chapter identifies some of the problems and discusses the relationships of these findings to the teaching of English.

Socioeconomic Status

The socioeconomic status (SES) of students is both the most investigated and the most difficult context variable to adjust to, especially for middle-class teachers working in communities with predominantly low SES students. The problem is compounded by the interaction of cultural and racial bias, since many of the urban poor are new immigrants, Hispanics, or Blacks. The research literature provides many examples of teachers reacting to students' ethnicity or race instead of to their actual ability or learning performance (Stulac 1982). The review of Brophy and Good (1974) revealed that white teachers gave less attention to black students and in some cases rejected and were hostile to bright black students. Simpson and Erickson (1983), studying the praise behavior of eight white and eight black first grade teachers in racially mixed urban classes, found that the white teachers directed more nonverbal criticism towards black males, whereas the black teachers were more neutral.

Teachers tend to adjust their teaching level to what they believe to be the learning level of the students and, because of stereotypic reactions to race or low SES, may freeze students in inappropriate tracks (Brophy and Good 1974). If tracking is done in kindergarten and first grade, then very often the only criterion is SES. Even though the difference between the low and high tracks in first grade may be only about seven months, by the third grade the spread is twenty months, and by tenth grade it may be seven years.

Some teachers react negatively to nonstandard English and to different nonverbal signals. For instance, middle-class teachers expect students to maintain eye contact during conversation as a sign of attention and respect, but students from other cultures such as Mexican and Asian may avert their eyes. Brophy and Good conclude that research shows children of higher SES tend to be in higher tracks and lower SES children in lower tracks, even if their measured ability indicates differently.

The research on expectation communication, commonly referred to as the Pygmalion studies, is very helpful in describing the nature of the expectations and offers ways to correct the resulting problems (Rosenthal and Jacobson 1968). Basically the process operates in the following manner:

1. Teacher expectations are inaccurate and inflexible.

2. The teacher then inaccurately sees some student characteristics and fails to see others.

3. The teacher treats the student as if he or she were someone else.

4. The teacher exerts pressure on the student to conform to the expectations.

5. This conforming behavior reinforces teacher expectations all the more.

6. The situation finally creates a behavior change in the student.

The process is interactive and dependent upon the teacher's first unreal expectation and the student's attempt to eventually agree (Brophy and Good 1974). Brophy and Good suggested that several contexts contribute to the possibility of a self-fulfilling prophecy: sex of student, behavior of student, teacher attitudes, and teacher expectancy. In a two-way exchange, students shape teacher behavior at the same time that their own behavior is being influenced by the teacher.

In a recent work by Cooper and Good (1983), the issue focused on loss of control and self-efficacy: "It seems [for lower students] that the effects of feeling little personal control, or specifically, little effort-outcome covariation, may be (1) negative affect and attitudes toward tasks presented, (2) less persistence in the face of failure, and (3) a greater incidence of failure." (22) Cooper and Good pointed out that the teachers who have rigid and unrealistic negative attitudes may be in the minority and may tend to be very insecure. In this study, the teachers directed more questions and praise toward high-expectation students and gave them less absolute criticism, but both absolute and relative praise showed diminishing expectation effects as the year progressed. The researchers found that high-expectation students retain a high success rate regardless of teacher interactional control. For low-expectation students, success may be seen as more dependent on the material involved, on the amount of time available, and on whether the teacher is prepared to expend the energy demanded by the interaction. Cooper and Good concluded that the more control a context affords the teacher, the greater the likelihood of a positive outcome. Thus teacher expectancy can be powerful, but not as direct as originally feared. It can be tempered by the experience of the teacher with the students, by support from the community and school administration, and by the individual pupil's resistance to the "prophecy."

Coming from the Pygmalion studies and the recent work on school and teacher effectiveness research, some findings suggest specific strategies to increase the school success of low SES and beginning students. In these studies, the causes of the need to differentiate teaching techniques between low and high SES students are not identified. Basically, the information is factual: schools with a high percentage of low SES students score lower in academic achievement than do schools with a high percentage of high SES students (Walberg and Rasher 1979).

The Beginning Teacher Evaluation Study (BTES) identified specific procedures used by teachers who were successful at increasing low SES students' academic learning time (Fisher, Filby, and Marliave 1977; Stallings 1978). In general, anything that decreases time on task for the student is to be avoided, and anything that increases time on task is to be encouraged. Brophy and Evertson (1974) found that low SES primary students require more directed instruction and teacher supervision to increase learning. In contrast, high SES primary students may successfully achieve with less direct teaching and structure. If one group were very successful with only certain styles of teaching, teacher effectiveness would prove to be a problem, especially if the teacher were unable to shift styles or if the low and the high SES groups were in equal proportions in a class.

Although recent major efforts on teacher effectiveness studies (for example, BTES and the Texas Teacher Effectiveness Study) have focused on the lower elementary grades, Stallings, Needels, and Stayrook (1979) studied secondary remedial reading classrooms and concluded that the students were quite similar to the low SES elementary students and require more teacher direction, praise, and interaction in order to achieve.

Unfortunately, children from low SES groups may have negative attitudes towards learning and school, which may show up in high absentee rates and high frequency of classroom disturbances. Swick and Hanley (1980), in their summary of research on stress, point out that discipline and classroom control are major sources of interpersonal stress for teachers. Other researchers previously mentioned have noted that time spent on managing discipline and maintaining class control is simply unproductive to learning (Fisher, Filby, and Marliave 1977). Teachers experience stress in trying to attend to the needs of many kinds of students at once, leading to reduced effectiveness, if not burnout.

Recent research suggests ways to help increase teacher effectiveness with low SES students. Several studies support the general practice of increasing the efficiency of time allocated to learning (Fisher, Filby, and Marliave 1977 in BTES; Stallings 1978 in Project Follow Through; Brophy and Evertson 1974; and Brookover et al. 1979). According to Brookover, an effective school is characterized by "high evaluations of students, high expectations, [and] high norms of achievement, with the appropriate patterns of reinforcement and instruction [in which students] acquire a sense of control over their environment and overcome feelings of futility which . . . characterize the students in many schools." (243)

The key factor in improving teacher effectiveness is administrative leadership and support of faculty and students (Rosenshine 1971; Ellett and Walberg 1979). Also, the research on teacher expectations points to the advisability of maintaining high, positive, but flexible expectations for all students (Cooper and Good 1983; Brophy and Good 1974). One study (Walberg, Boll, and Waxman 1977 [cited in Marjoribanks 1979]) in which a one-year program was aimed at training parents to create conditions in the home to facilitate academic achievement was successful in increasing the children's reading scores (1.1 grade gain, compared with 0.5 gain in the control classes).

In summary, the pupil property of socioeconomic status offers a powerful context for teacher effectiveness. It establishes areas of concern that cut across grade levels, race, sex, and content and affects teacher and student morale, parent satisfaction, and community approval of schools. These studies suggest that special differential teaching techniques may be required to work with the low and the high SES groups in the early elementary and remedial classes. Parent training programs could be very helpful, and supportive administrative policies are needed to increase teacher effectiveness. Since the educational level of the parents is a key variable in determining the SES of a pupil, the increase of educational opportunity for all citizens in a community could break the chain for the next generation and should be encouraged as an educational goal.

Community Attitudes towards School

Research on community-school relationships is closely linked to the research on socioeconomic status. Generally, the higher the SES, the more involvement with schools and schoolwork. The study by Haertel et al. (1981) of National Assessment of Educational Progress results on science found increased motivation in science with higher SES. The authors suggested that family support and self-expectations are prerequisites for high science motivation. Haertel et al. agreed with Walberg and Rasher (1979), who concluded after their analyses of school achievement in fifty states that schooling does make a difference in upgrading society. The students whose parents have received higher levels of formal education do achieve more and are more responsive in turn to the educational needs of their children.

Recent studies of leisure reading, homework, and television viewing offer insights into the need for parental control over children's leisure-time activities. Rosenshine and Berliner's (1978) summary of research on academic engaged time indicated a significant relationship between the amount of time engaged in reading and students' scores on reading achievement. In contrast, the studies of television viewing do not support increased achievement. Williams et al. (1982) found that televiewing, overall, has a slightly negative effect on school achievement and that the effects are not linear. Up to ten hours a week may result in increased achievement, more than ten hours is detrimental. The impact was significantly greater on girls' achievement than on boys' and on high IQ students than low or medium.

In the 1979–80 and 1980–81 Annual Reports of Student Achievement in California Schools from the California State Department of Education (Fetler 1982), the data for both sixth grade and twelfth grade students show that increased televiewing is correlated with lower scores on reading, math, and written expression in all of the SES groups analyzed. The data also show that increased leisure reading and homework correlate positively with increased scores in all SES groups. Fetler found that moderate viewing was associated with relatively higher achievement for low SES students. These studies point out that television is not the archenemy. The problem simply is that too much television leaves no time for intellectual stimulation from leisure reading and homework.

Wolf (1979) reported that the homework load in the United States is about half that in other countries. As so many studies from the Beginning Teacher Evaluation Study have pointed out, the quality of a student's performance in school is closely tied to the time allowed for learning and the opportunity for learning. Communities and families are strong influences on the propensity that young people have for dropping out of school. For the young men, economic necessity may force them to enter the labor market and drop out of school. For the young women, pregnancies and economic necessity may be the immediate reasons for dropping out (Rumberger 1983), thus beginning a new cycle of children who may also drop out in their early adolescence.

Intervention programs to build family and community awareness of ways to help students succeed in school have been successful. Walberg (1982) concluded about home climate and school success: "The educational stimulation and social-psychological supportiveness of the student in the home by the parents are more closely linked to learning and self-concept development than are social class indexes and the number of children in the family." (302) Fantini (1982), in summarizing recent research on community and school success, stated two tentative conclusions: first, that participation of parents in school governance shows no significant impact on school achievement (except for the self-concept of the child whose parent is participating) and, second, that the use of parents in the educational process as paraprofessionals and educators does show a relationship to school achievement in reading and mathematics, as well as to improved self-concept. The Chicago studies of Conrad and Eash (1983) and Walberg, Bole, and Waxman (1977) identify positive programs involving the parents both at home and in school that have resulted in improved academic success for their children.

In summary, the power that the family-community has on the success of children in school seems clear. Recent research suggests that if students are to succeed academically, educators must convince parents to control the use of children's free time so that homework, leisure reading, and a moderate amount of television can be in balance. Programs to bring the community and parents into the schools are also important in reversing the negative effects of low SES on teacher-school effectiveness.

Gender Differences

Just as the socioeconomic status and race of students may influence a teacher's effectiveness, so also may the sex and physical appearance of students. Brophy and Good (1974) suggest that elementary schools are possibly better suited to the needs and interests of girls than of boys. The ideal behavior rewarded by most elementary teachers is passive and compliant behavior, which does not correspond to the more active behavior of young boys (Good and Brophy 1973; Brophy and Good 1974). Boys tend to get more criticism, harsher tones, and sometimes lower grades than their performance warrants. Perhaps as a result, girls tend to have a more favorable attitude towards school than boys do. However, Simpson and Erickson (1983), in a study of sixteen first grade classrooms, found out that white teachers gave more verbal praise to boys than to girls, but the boys also received more verbal criticism.

The running debate on sex differences and achievement in school still continues. Haertel et al. (1981) report on the following: (1) *General intelligence*—girls perform better during preschool; boys perform better in high school. (2) *Verbal ability*—girls are better at grammar, spelling, and word fluency, but after age ten the difference between girls and boys is not large. (3) *Math*—there is no difference in the early years, but after age fourteen, boys outperform girls in arithmetic and spatial ability. (4) *Analytic ability*—boys are slightly higher. (5) *Problem solving*—when a solution requires manipulation of objects and trying a wide range of approaches, boys outperform girls, otherwise boys and girls are fairly even. (6) *School grades*—girls get better grades at all levels, even in subjects where boys may excel on standardized tests.

Haertel et al. (1981) analyzed the National Assessment of Educational Progress data on science learning and did not find any difference between the sexes. The data did show, however, increased motivation for boys of higher SES. Haertel cited Walberg's (1967) study of science ability with the Harvard Project Physics students, which revealed that the girls outscored the boys on three of five dimensions: boys were better at tinkering and cosmology, while girls were better at academics, nature study, and applied life. Walberg suggests that cultural stereotyping may be responsible. Hannafin (1983), in a study of the math skills of sixth grade Anglo and Hispanic students, found no difference between boys and girls. Along with the increasing evidence of the power of culture to influence potential achievement in math and science dependent upon sex, Brophy and Good (1974) reviewed studies from Brazil, England, Italy, and Germany. They found that boys in those countries do not have as many reading difficulties as boys appear to have in the United States. The authors suggested that the problem may be a result of the predominance of female teachers in elementary school, and young boys' perception of reading as feminine.

Sex differences may certainly affect teacher effectiveness, especially in reading during elementary school and in science and math during secondary school. Children do not always do as expected, however, and teachers may not always prejudge a student's ability based only on sex.

Student Attitudes towards School, Teachers, Subject, and Self

What influence does the student's own attitude have on teacher effectiveness? Can a teacher be effective with students who have negative attitudes towards school, teachers, the subjects, and self? Work on the Pygmalion studies (Brophy and Good 1974) identified a wide range of individual interactions in the classroom and suggested that the students shape teacher behavior while their own behavior is being shaped by the teacher. Students who have a poor self-concept and who are in a fail cycle very often respond to an external "locus of control" (Peterson and Walberg 1979) and respond best to directed teaching techniques as opposed to inquiry or other open techniques.

Rosenshine and Berliner (1978) explain that "many students do not engage in on-task behavior when a teacher or another adult is not monitoring their academic activities." Thus the traditional large group instruction practice of directed teaching simply provides for better supervision. On the other hand, Peterson and Walberg (1979) report that students taught with open approaches were more independent and curious, and had better attitudes towards school and teachers than students taught with directed techniques. This conclusion corresponds with a common finding in "open" versus "traditional" classroom research, in that the students achieve about the same under both styles but the attitudes of students in the open classroom are more positive.

On the specific negative attitude effects of absenteeism, researchers are not clear. In a study by Harris et al. (1968), higher rates of absenteeism appeared to correlate significantly with lower scores on reading achievement. And Rosenshine (1971) reported similar correlations in three of four studies. The fourth study did not show such a correlation. The inconsistency of these findings in studies of inner-city first and second grade students is puzzling, but the direction of correlation may indicate a negative effect of absenteeism on reading achievement.

In a later study by Fredrick et al. (1976), the use of class time in 175 eleventh grade classrooms was studied in Chicago and correlated with reading scores. The results showed that the schools with higher reading achievement scores had a lower amount of lost time and more reinforcing comments by teachers. The other finding was that throughout the schools an extraordinarily high proportion of class time was lost (an average of 46.5 percent) to absences, lateness, inattention, interruptions, and non-involvement. Although teacher effectiveness was not specifically designated as a variable in the study, it seems logical to assume that such high percentages of lost time correlating with the low reading scores points to a direct impact on teacher effectiveness.

Recommendations

Certainly, teachers who have worked for many years in communities have learned effective ways of reaching the pupils of those communities. These teachers have much to give others, and institutes should be funded to provide them with an opportunity to share their expertise, perhaps in a manner similar to the Bay Area Writing Project. However, the problem remains that most teachers come from middle-class, educated families and may not understand how to reach children whose most important concern may be survival. Many young teachers burn out quickly and leave the profession when they are unsuccessful with such children. Recent research has provided the teaching profession with useful insights that should bring about a better-trained cadre of beginning teachers. With the help of professional organizations, local and state educational agencies, and teacher training institutions, the entire profession should be improved to better serve our schools.

The research reviewed in this section supports the following suggestions for improvement:

1. Both in-service and pre-service teachers should be thoroughly trained in a wide range of teaching methods and should be aware of the appropriateness and limitations of each method for the various levels and ability groups of children.

2. Schools should form site committees to develop parent training programs to improve home environments for student learning.

3. Programs for improving interpersonal communications need to be established for all teachers and especially for those working in multiethnic schools.

4. School districts and universities need to provide ongoing training to assist teachers in improving classroom management skills to improve student discipline and time on task.

Summary

The research on contextual factors related to the community identifies several major sources of interference with teaching effectiveness. Teachers may be influenced negatively by students from low SES communities or by their race or ethnicity. Teachers may adjust their expectations of students on the basis of their stereotypes about race, ethnicity, SES, and language. Students who are assigned to tracks in the early years or to special classes may not be reevaluated properly so that they can attend regular classes, even if the original assignments were inappropriate. Fortunately, the studies also indicated that teacher awareness, as well as support from school and community, can modify the negative effects toward more favorable outcomes.

Students from remedial classes in low SES communities may function better with direct instruction styles than with indirect or open styles. In practice, a direct style might include more teacher-directed lessons, direct supervision, teacher praise, basic English and remedial classes at all levels, and less reliance on individual seatwork and small group work using peer leaders. In contrast, the higher SES classes could use indirect and open approaches in regular elementary and secondary English language arts classes. Basically, careful monitoring of students, teacher awareness of bias and special attitudes, and seeking a balanced mode of instruction suitable for the makeup and content of the class would be advisable tactics.

Working in low SES schools that have many student discipline problems is a major source of stress for teachers. Stress often results in burnout, illness, and resignation from teaching. The policies and subsequent follow-through by administrators in charge of an educational unit are key factors that show up in these studies in managing discipline. Especially crucial is the ability of the administrative leadership to unite the efforts of the total school community in agreed-upon disciplinary goals. Effective schools were identified as places where the students assume responsibility for developing policies within the school. The contact between home and school is also critical, and several studies identified programs where the home environment for education was successfully improved by cooperative efforts between school and home. Such things as absence from school and overuse of television will result in low academic performance, especially in English, math, and science. These are some areas that can be addressed by school-home programs in low SES communities.

Teachers may be influenced by the sex of their students and thus treat boys and girls differently. Although sexual bias may be a common pattern, the research shows that differences in academic achievement related to sex are largely mythical or dependent upon cultural patterns and teacher expectations.

The Context of Policy

Teacher effectiveness in English or in any other subject is not only modified by the interaction of pupil properties with content and teaching strategies, but also by the policy decisions of legislators, state departments of education, universities, local school boards, school administrators, local school committees, and departments. These policies may enhance or strangle the work of teachers. The effects of several policies have been discussed in the previous section on community context, specifically, student discipline and administrative support for teachers (or the lack of such support).

This section will review the results of selected studies on the effects that policies have on teachers and the physical conditions in which they work. Since policies are generally legal descriptions of actions and since most involve finances, the policy context will be discussed only as it applies to the human or physical dimension. In this section, the discussion will also be concerned with policymakers outside the English teaching profession. The discussion will deal with school climate, class size, homogeneity of students within classes, and conditions of the workplace.

School Climate

The Pygmalion studies deal with the possible influence of the teacher's expectations on student achievement. Similarly, the recent research on school effectiveness deals with the possible influences that school principals, administrative policies, and actions have on how effective teachers are in helping students achieve. A study of the teaching of French in 122 English schools is an interesting example. Burstall (1968, cited in Rosenshine 1971) found that a high proportion of successful but low-ability students attended schools where the head teacher (principal) scored above the mean on a test of opinion on whether French should be taught to students of low ability. The classroom teachers, responding to the head teacher's attitude, maintained positive attitudes themselves.

More recently, Ellett and Walberg (1979) in writing about Project ROME in Georgia schools concluded: "In schools where the principal is performing important behaviors in the school environment, teachers' attitudes toward a variety of work related dimensions are positive and often show strong connections with student outcomes." (158) Purkey and Smith (1983), summarizing a study of reading achievement in six schools conducted by Trisman and associates (1976), found that effective schools are characterized by the principal's strong instructional leadership, high expectations for student achievement, good school atmosphere, a clear focus on basic skills and small group instruction, and interchange of ideas among the staff. After reviewing a decade of school effectiveness research, Purkey and Smith concluded: "Most schools with effective programs are characterized by high staff expectations and morale, a considerable degree of control by the staff over instruction and training decisions in the school, clear leadership from the principal, clear goals for the school, and a sense of order in the school." (438)

The school effectiveness research and the BTES research clearly point to the need for strong administrative policies and actions to enable the school to function as a place where efficient learning can take place. School discipline is essential to increase academic learning time. Administrative practices such as interrupting classes for announcements, pulling students out for extracurricular activities, permissive policies on absence, lateness, and class disruption result in lost time for instruction (Frederick et al. 1976) and high stress for the teachers (Pettegrew and Wolf 1982), which lead to low morale and possible teacher burnout.

Chichon and Koff (1978) identified four of the most stressful events for teachers: (1) involuntary transfer, (2) disruptive students, (3) notice of unsatisfactory work performance, and (4) physical threats from students. All of these events are concerned with administrative policies and actions. In a like vein, Golladay and Noell (1978) identified problems that hinder teachers' work: (1) student discipline, (2) student attitudes, (3) incompetent administration, (4) heavy work loads, and (5) lack of resources. Again, administrative policy heavily influences the nature of these problems.

From their studies of the stress factors related to teaching, Kryiacou and Sutcliffe (1977) suggested that stress within the profession is considerable and may have far-reaching consequences for the entire system of public education. Kahn et al. (1964) stated that the high level of stress experienced by teachers is tied directly to organizational effectiveness and management practices. Stress may result when teachers are forced to accept unfamiliar teaching styles, are omitted from the decision-making process, and have no support or even social interactions with other adults at the school (Armstrong 1983).

The principal's influence may be considerable in the ultimate realization of teacher effectiveness in the classroom. However, ineffective teaching practices, faulty relationships among teachers and students, and community attitudes and relationships with the school are equally powerful. The principal is only one key element in the complex organization of a school (Ellett and Walberg 1979). Perhaps a useful way of considering the effect that all key elements in a school have on teacher effectiveness is to look at a school as "a loosely coupled system" rather than as a bureaucratic hierarchy susceptible to rational control and with high responsiveness at the teacher-student level. Brookover et al. (1979, cited in Purkey and Smith 1983) theorized that student achievement is strongly affected by a school's "social system" or culture. The social system actually varies from school to school and even within similar subsamples where the SES and racial composition were controlled. Brookover suggested that three variables operate to make up the school structure:

1. Social inputs (student body, faculty, staff)

2. Structure (school size, open or closed classrooms)

3. Climate (school culture, expectations of students, faculty, administration, feelings about the school)

Purkey and Smith (1983) concluded that the best strategy for changing a school involves collaborative planning and collegial work to develop an atmosphere conducive to experimentation and evaluation. Little (1982) described what four successful schools did that was different from the unsuccessful schools. The teachers valued and participated in collegiality and continuous improvement (experimentation). They also interacted professionally with fellow teachers and administrators through shop talk and shared planning, and they did structured observations. Purkey and

Smith (1983), referring to the Rutter et al. (1979) study of twelve inner city schools in London from 1970 to 1974, described the effective schools as having the following characteristics:

1. Class management that kept students actively engaged in learning activities

2. Classrooms in which praise was given freely and discipline applied frequently and firmly

3. A general expectation for academic success coupled with specific actions emphasizing those attitudes

4. Students given responsibility for personal and school duties

5. Immediate feedback to students on what is acceptable performance

6. Staff consensus on the values and aims of the school as a whole

7. Clearly recognizable principles and guidelines of student behavior

8. A clean, comfortable, and well-maintained physical environment for students

9. Staff concern for student welfare

10. Treatment of students emphasizing their success and potential

The researchers found that these effective schools had higher school attendance, less delinquency, and higher student achievement.

The BTES researchers emphasize how crucial it is that the teaching staff be involved in increasing time on task, improving diagnostic and prescriptive skills, improving teacher-student interaction, monitoring teachers, giving them feedback, and improving cooperation and student responsibility (Noli 1980). Purkey and Smith (1983) reviewed the past decade of studies in school effectiveness research and suggested that new directions have emerged for school improvement. The new directions include increasing classroom time (Fisher et al. 1980), creating an improved school atmosphere (Weber 1971), and district allowance of school site management (Hargrove et al. 1981).

Purkey and Smith further synthesized this research by listing four variables for success: (1) collaborative planning and collegial relationships, (2) sense of community, (3) clear goals and high expectations commonly shared, and (4) order and discipline. (444-45) They emphasized that "teachers and administrators who cannot or will not strive for the academic success of every student have no place in schools that choose to stress learning cognitive skills." (447) Thus the relationship of school climate to teacher effectiveness appears to be both direct and highly complex. Administrative policies may create improvement or breakdown. Involving the teaching staff in crucial areas of decision making seems to be essential for improving the chances of significant student achievement.

Class Size

For the past seventy years, the National Council of Teachers of English has proclaimed an optimum of twenty students per class, or no more than one hundred students per day, as the limit for regular English classes. Little reference has been made to special classes for advanced students or for those of low ability,* but several recommendations have been made over the years to designate a low class size for those groups. Nowhere has either NCTE or the International Reading Association advocated class sizes of thirty-five to forty for English, language arts, or reading classes, yet English and reading classrooms continue to be filled to those levels in districts all across the United States.

Unfortunately, the research on class size has not dramatically shown the deleterious effects on student achievement. Such studies found "no significant difference," and administrators reading those results assumed no great harm would be done by increasing class size. Very little formal research on teacher attitudes and effectiveness related to class size was done. However, in English the damage of large classes showed up in the form of changes in composition and literature study. Teachers had to curtail, and in some classes stop assigning, written compositions altogether. The appalling scores on composition performance may have been a result. Recent studies on class size appear to be proving the position taken by NCTE years ago. The error on the part of researchers may have been related to the use of criterion measures of superficial educational achievement rather than on measures of deeper understanding (Kuert 1979).

In a recent two-year study of sixty-two classes in grades 4 and 5, Shapson et al. (1980) explored the effects that classes of sixteen, twenty-three, thirty, and thirty-seven students had on teacher expectations and the attitudes of teachers and students, as well as on student achievement in reading, math, composition, and art. Although the teachers' expectations of class size were confirmed by their experience, the actual results of a student performance failed to support their opinions. Some gain was realized in math with small classes, but not in other subjects (including reading and composition), nor in students' self-concepts and attitudes. Shapson et al. also observed that the teachers *did not vary* their teaching

---

*An exception is the reference to remedial or developmental classes that appears in NCTE's *Guidelines for the Workload of the College English Teacher* (1987). This recommendation calls for a maximum enrollment of fifteen students per section.

technique, no matter what the size of the class. This study demonstrated that, within a range of sixteen to thirty-seven students and specifically at grade levels 4 and 5, class size makes a large difference to teachers but little difference to students or to the instructional methods used.

Using meta-analysis techniques, Glass and Smith (1978; Glass and Smith 1980) analyzed the data of eighty studies in 1978–79 and fifty-nine studies in 1980. The analysis revealed the small but consistent effects of class size. The analysis showed positive effects on achievement, and substantial relationships between class size on the one hand and teacher and pupil attitudes on the other. The effects on the teachers were favorable in the areas of work load, morale, and attitude towards students, and on students in the areas of self-concept, interest in school, and class participation. Smaller classes were associated with greater attempts to individualize and to provide better classroom climate.

Glass and Smith (1978) studied class sizes ranging from five to seventy and concluded that "as class size increases, achievement decreases. A pupil who would score at about the 63rd percentile on a national test when taught individually, would score at about the 37th percentile in a class of 40 pupils. The difference in being in a class of 20 versus a class of 40 is an advantage of 10 percentile ranks. . . . Few resources at the command of educators will reliably produce effects of that magnitude." (i) In a different approach to the Glass and Smith meta-analysis, Hedges and Stock (1983) concluded that "the results of our analysis suggest that the use of suboptimal statistical methods did not greatly affect the results of the meta-analysis by Glass and Smith" (63), thus supporting the findings of the Glass and Smith meta-analysis.

Walberg and Rasher (1979), in writing about educational achievement in the United States, found that "despite the variation in expenditure per pupil from $586 in Mississippi to $2,084 in Florida, expenditures bear no relation to rate of failure when controlled for population characteristics; yet the pupil-teacher ratio, varying from 26.8 in Utah to 17.0 in Vermont, does. A reduction of one pupil per teacher is associated with an estimated 7.9 percent reduction in rate of failure when the other variables are controlled." (358) Walberg and Rasher suggest that even though capital expenses to support small classes would be necessary, small classes would pay off because of the intensified and direct services that teachers would be able to provide for children.

It is important to note that the Glass and Smith study dealt with many subject fields. According to professional opinion and experience, English and reading are specifically in need of small class sizes. A meta-analysis of class size by level and subject would assist the English profession greatly in its realization of a seventy-year-old recommendation on working conditions.

Homogeneity of Students

The issue of whether ability grouping increases student achievement has been the subject of raging debate in educational research for many years. Generally, researchers from the behavioral sciences urge heterogeneous grouping, while teachers and administrators favor homogeneous grouping. After reviewing research on ability grouping, Good and Brophy (1973) concluded that "the evidence simply indicates that ability grouping *per se* tends to be ineffective and does more harm than good." (249) They see dangers leading to the misteaching of students and the failure of low-ability students to progress.

Brophy and Good (1974) pointed out that high-track students are likely to come from high SES homes, that teachers working with these students have higher morale and enthusiasm, and that high-track students provide more intellectual stimulation for each other. On the other hand, low-track students often get the poorest resources the school has to offer, and the achievement difference between the two groups widens dramatically as they progress through the grades. Teachers also adjust their level to what they believe to be the level of the students.

Teacher attitudes towards tracking, however, are quite different. Although many of the research findings are contradictory and inconclusive, a common finding is that homogeneous grouping benefits high-achieving students, and heterogeneous grouping is socially beneficial to low-achieving students. Although teacher effectiveness is not usually identified as an outcome, it is informally inferred from the academic performance of the students.

In a study of 403 teachers in London secondary schools, Reid et al. (1981) found that 92 percent considered heterogeneous classes to be of some advantage for students, and 75 percent saw some advantage for teachers. Fifty-nine percent felt that mixed grouping slowed the able students down, forcing the teacher to accept a lower standard of work. Finally, 45 percent of the teachers saw problems for the less able because the teaching was geared to the middle level, leaving the slow student behind. The teachers agreed that mixed grouping increased the demands on the teacher, increased teacher stress, required more resources, increased preparation and marking, and required small class sizes. In general, the teachers felt that mixed ability grouping was good for physical education, integrated humanities, and aesthetic subjects, but not good for math, language studies, and science.

Evertson, Sanford, and Emmer (1981) studied twenty-seven junior high English classes in a metropolitan district for the 1978–79 school year. The results suggested that heterogeneity of students' achievement levels when entering a given class puts limits on a teacher's ability to successfully adapt instruction to an individual student's academic and affective needs. The classes with a wider range of heterogeneity were associated with a lower degree of student engagement and cooperation. These findings confirm other observations that teachers must pay more attention to discipline and management in English classes of mixed ability. Evertson found a significant negative correlation ($R = -.33$) between percentage of low entering achievement with expected gains and class heterogeneity. In English classes, extreme heterogeneity may be a handicap to lower-ability students.

Evertson's study identified five strategies that more successful teachers use in heterogeneously grouped classes:

1. Special attention and in-class assistance to lower ability students in class

2. Limited use of within-class ability groupings and differentiation of materials or assignments

3. Differential grading (taking individual student levels and progress into consideration)

4. Limited use of peer tutoring

5. Frequent academic feedback to all students in class

6. High levels of student accountability for written work and class participation.

Evertson concluded that heterogeneous grouping in junior high English classes places extraordinary demands on teachers' time, attention, and classroom management skills, and that even in the hands of skilled classroom managers the extreme classes were less than ideal learning environments. Brophy (1983) discussed the discipline problems of slow students and suggested the techniques of using special individualized tutoring, contracts, and study carrels or special quiet places for distractible students.

In a recent meta-analysis of fifty-two studies of secondary schools, Kulik and Kulik (1982) found that homogeneous grouping increased criterion scores from 50 to 54 percent for a typical student. The study also revealed that the size of the effect differed in different groups. Honor classes produced clear effects, whereas average and below-average groups produced near zero effects. However, the students in all ability groups developed more positive attitudes towards the subjects they were studying than did the students in the ungrouped classes.

From these studies it seems logical to conclude tentatively that homogeneous grouping in English would improve teacher effectiveness by reducing the work load, management problems, and the resultant stress. Homogeneous grouping would also improve student achievement by providing a better academic fit and work satisfaction.

The Workplace and Conditions of Practice

The conditions of the workplace where teachers are expected to be effective are often unsatisfactory, but are usually quite easily corrected. Unfortunately, a well-ingrained but unofficial tradition of "hazing" goes on in many schools where beginning teachers are given undesirable classes, multiple preparations, and several classroom assignments throughout the day. In addition, new teachers may be assigned classes they have not been academically trained to teach and may receive little or no support or guidance from either the faculty or the administrators (Armstrong 1983). With such practices ensuring failure in teacher effectiveness, young teachers often leave the profession, especially creative, bright people who can have their choice of careers.

Even with the best of teaching assignments—a single classroom, reasonable assignment of classes, and within the parameters of the chosen academic field—many schools are depressing, unattractive, prisonlike institutions with schedules so tight that it is difficult to relax or even to perform natural biological functions. McGuffey (1982) summarized the relatively small body of research in this area: "The lack of a single coordinated research organization with concern for the impact of the total physical environment on education and on the learner in educational settings may continue to hamper more comprehensive approaches to research on educational facilities." (238)

McGuffey's findings from recent research include the following points:

1. The achievement of students assigned to modern school buildings is consistently higher than that of students assigned to older buildings.

2. Temperatures above 80 degrees produce harmful physiological effects that decrease work efficiency.

3. Students learn better in the winter.

4. Bad lighting leads to ineffective information collecting and physical discomfort.

5. Schools painted according to the principles of color dynamics seem to result in greater improvement for the students.

6. Beautiful colors stimulate activity and alertness.

7. Carpeting has a very positive effect on learning. Noise distresses and distracts.

8. Open-space and underground schools result in about the same achievement as traditional schools.

The variance for each of these areas on school achievement is relatively small, but the accumulation of variance effects may provide another view of the impact of these facilities variables. It may be doubly significant that only one of the seventy-eight references cited in McGuffey's extensive review actually deals with the effect on the teacher. Yet the teacher may spend forty years working in a school environment and may be negatively affected by the accumulation of environmental conditions.

Summary and Implications

The context of policy and its effects go far beyond the examples presented in this section. For example, the specific changes in curriculum generated by PL 194 (mainstreaming), the effects of California's SB 813 on school reform, or tax laws such as California's Proposition 13 were not discussed. Also, the effects of textbook selection committees at local and state levels and the usual publishers' race to conform in order to enhance sales were not discussed here. Nor were the efforts of pressure groups to censor textbooks and control curriculum considered. Davis's (1979) publication contains an excellent discussion of the seriousness of censorship in the United States and offers direction for the English teaching profession on the matter of special interest groups and curriculum.

These selected studies, however, do illustrate the power of policy to affect teaching. The schools where the entire staff participates in making decisions and administrators follow through in implementing the policies are the effective ones, whether they are in a low, middle, or high SES community. The morale of the faculty and the achievement of the students are higher in these schools than in schools where cooperative decision making is lacking and where agreed-upon policies are not implemented. English teachers in particular are more effective in schools that have firm policies on absence, lateness, and class disruptions and where the bureaucratic paper work can be lightened.

The school climate is affected not only by official policies of the district and local administration but by the subtle yet powerful impact of the school culture—a kind of informal policy determined by longstanding tradition about what goes on at the school. Simply by walking around various campuses of secondary schools, one can pick up some noticeable similarities and differences among the schools. These differences have the power to drastically affect the policies governing curriculum decisions made at the school, department, and class level, thereby affecting the learning level and attitudes of the students. For example, if the boys decide that carrying books is not socially desirable, then the teachers may find it impossible to use homework assignments as a strategy for learning. This would then necessarily decrease the amount of time that students spend on learning and would affect the teacher's curriculum decisions. In English classes in schools that have this informal policy, it may be impossible to study more than one major novel a semester—if that much. In this situation, the usual strategy is to concentrate on short fiction, short plays, and some poetry.

It seems necessary, then, for the English teaching profession to promote multidisciplinary, multifaceted studies of the school climate and its resultant impact on the English program. A strong, persistent program of collaborative planning—involving community, faculty, administration, and students—is essential for developing the positive aspects of school climate. English teachers should also become aware of the specific characteristics of the climate at their respective schools and determine effective strategies to compensate.

The jury may be still out on the effects of class size on learning; however, we are encouraged by the results of the new meta-analysis studies showing the negative effect of class size on student learning. What we have not seen in the literature is a clearly described study of the impact that large classes have on English teachers over a long period of time. From the classic study by Dusel (1955), we have some idea of the effect that an overload has on the average time spent marking a composition. Most English teachers are bitterly aware of the thousands of extra hours spent in grading and marking the compositions of those extra students. The persistent practice of using exercises in traditional grammar probably stems from the reluctance of overloaded teachers to assign compositions. The makers of policy are not listening to the English teaching profession. We need to mount a more active political campaign for change.

One way to help teachers manage the large class load in English may be to use homogeneous grouping or tracking. Basically, researchers and psychologists are against homogeneous grouping, but working teachers, especially in secondary English, support it. Policy decisions in support of homogeneous grouping might be important for individual classes in the English program, whereas general tracking in grades 1 through 12 should be discouraged.

Unfortunately, the practice of hazing new English teachers is widespread, even though the administration responsible would certainly deny intentional hazing. Far too many new English teachers begin their careers with more than two preparations in several classrooms and are often responsible for courses they have never taught or have never been prepared to teach. The notion still seems to persist that anyone who can speak English is able to teach it.

We have buildings that are improperly heated or, in the case of warm climates, have no air conditioning. We have classrooms with prisonlike atmospheres, unadorned by colors and textures that might create a more favorable climate for education. Joint efforts on the part of teachers, students, administrators, and community to improve the physical plant of the school and to create a sense of community within it should be strongly encouraged.

The basic realization coming from reviewing the research dealing with the context of policy and teacher effectiveness is that policy decisions may have an insidious control over the work of teachers. All teachers must therefore mount concerted efforts to develop useful and enabling policies.

The Context of Profession

Context is operationally defined in this report as those aspects that "concern the conditions to which teachers must adjust." In this section, the context of profession and selected research on the teacher, the department, and the larger profession will be discussed in relation to teacher effectiveness.

English Training

Pre-service training specific to the preparation of English teachers has been described in chapter 2 of this monograph. As a context to which a teacher must adjust, pre-service training may or may not be helpful in the development of an effective English teacher. In the United States, the patterns for training programs in the universities and school districts vary, ranging from almost no training to intern or M.A. programs of one or two years. Along with the variation of training time, there are varied emphases and contents. Even the academic courses that English majors take to prepare for a B.A. degree vary considerably from university to university.

In most instances, these academic programs bear little resemblance to the subject of English and English language arts as actually taught by elementary and secondary teachers. We assume that the scholarly studies found in most college English departments provide some grounding for a prospective teacher. But far too often, the bright young teacher comes to an assignment after a rich experience with literary studies, only to be assigned to teach junior high school English or English as a second language. Contrary to the notions of some people, our profession is not the same as that of the university scholar or literary critic. The advanced courses in English at most universities are usually intended to prepare students for specialized graduate work in English. Unfortunately, specialization tends to be a continuing pattern in our major universities, even at the undergraduate level, where literature is separated from composition, linguistics, communications, and journalism. With this preparation in hand, prospective English teachers are immediately trapped by a competency problem—they simply do not know the content they are expected to teach. In desperation, even after having had English methods courses and student teaching, new teachers usually fall back on past impressions of English teaching, very often modeling themselves after teachers they never liked. New teachers also tend to accept the practices in vogue at their school and then rigidly follow them. Thus they assign grammar exercises instead of teaching composition, rely upon literal comprehension questions for instruction in literature, and fall back on spelling and vocabulary lists unrelated to literature study, even though professional leadership rejects these practices as ineffective (Rosenholtz 1985; Bolster 1983).

The Department

Departmental and administrative decisions and practices may have an important impact on the effectiveness of the teacher, for at this level the actual assignments—or misassignments, as the case may be—are made. Unfortunately, administrators often assume that a teacher can teach at any level and that similar teaching practices are appropriate for all school subjects. The research reviewed below provides new evidence for challenging such administrative practice.

Departmental decisions involve level and grade assignments for teachers, subject assignments, and text selection. These topics are therefore significant in maintaining teacher effectiveness. An individual teacher may have had excellent preparation in English and outstanding experience at the high school level and yet be sadly incompetent with a class of seventh grade students. Robinson (1985) reported on a growing problem, that of teachers from other fields being assigned to teach English. In the state of Washington, for example, according to a 1983-84 state agency report, 61 percent of the English classes were being taught out of field, and in high schools, 30 percent. The irony is that, at the time of this writing, English is one of the subjects that has an excess of job applicants in the state.

Grade Differences

That children behave differently throughout their formal schooling is a fact that anyone having even a minimal experience with schools would acknowledge. Brophy (1983) divided the school years into the following four differentiated stages characterized by specific student behavior and requiring different teaching strategies:

Stage I (K–3)	Students are mostly compliant and need to learn a student's role. They need much formal instruction about rules, classroom procedures, and routines.
Stage II (2–6)	Having learned the school rules, most students remain compliant. Teachers spend less time managing behavior.
Stage III (5–10)	Students seek attention and peer acceptance and are often resentful of authority. Horseplay is common, and class management is more time-consuming.
Stage IV (9–12)	Students are personally settled, and classrooms are more academic and businesslike. Management takes less time.

Problems occur, however, when students in one stage behave as if they were in another stage or when a teacher whose style is ideally suited for one level is assigned to another level. Problems can often occur, too, when a high school English teacher is assigned to remedial reading with students who may still be at stage I but show the emotional characteristics and behavior of stage III.

The recent work of BTES (Filby and Cahen 1978), Project Follow Through (Stallings 1975), and the Texas Teacher Effectiveness study (Brophy and Evertson 1974) supports the practices of positive feedback and heavy teacher support, along with direct teaching, using low-level questions, and providing frequent overt and active practice for remedial students. Rosenshine (1983) concluded from recent studies that, in general, students taught from a structured curriculum do better than with individualized or discovery learning approaches. Moreover, those who receive instruction from the teacher do better than those who receive coaching from groups or peers.

The differences from grade to grade are also compounded by the progressively increasing difference between the high-achieving student and the low-achieving student. In a single heterogeneous English class, the students may vary from grades 2 to 12 in achievement. Even the use of ability grouping may not resolve the issue, especially if a teacher is assigned extreme levels and tries to use the same techniques in both classes.

In a study of 362 junior high and 525 senior high classrooms, Sirotnik (1982) found that in senior high, grouping styles that have students work alone less often and that use upper-track classes tend to be associated with more time spent on instruction. In junior high classrooms, the grouping styles that have students in upper-track classes work alone more often were associated with less time spent on behavior problems and more time spent on instruction. These findings suggest a very real difference between successful styles at the two grade levels.

Loree (1965) explored the differences in the problem-solving techniques used by successful and unsuccessful students at grades 4 and 9. He found that the older children were superior in the possession and retrieval of information. They were better at extracting information and better at combining operations. His study also revealed very rapid improvement in these problem-solving operations up to grade 7, but almost no improvement in grades 8 and 9. The content areas concerned were social studies and science, which typically have a heavy input of information in the junior high years. Loree found that the weak problem-solvers had poorer motivation, no persistence, and negative attitudes. The weak students often did not understand the question, and although they may have had information, they were unable to use it effectively. Their structuring abilities were poor, and they also lacked the ability to verbalize. Thus, these studies point out that real differences exist from grade to grade between low- and high-ability students in their learning patterns, and, we assume, in their receptivity to different teaching styles.

Medley (1977) found that effective teachers in the upper grades talk more, keep pupils on task more, are less permissive, question at lower cognitive levels, have pupils approach the teacher, manage the classroom unobtrusively, and use fewer traditional materials than do the less effective teachers.

It appears that differences do exist in the appropriateness of teaching styles for various grade levels and between high-ability and low-ability students. A successful teacher at one grade level will not necessarily be successful at another, especially without sufficient time and training to learn effective techniques. The need for further research is still crucial for developing optimum techniques for working with students of varying learning styles. Perhaps we also need to use the results of past research to modify the methods practiced in the schools.

Subject Differences

The second major area to be discussed under the context of departmental and administrative units is the topic of subject differences and a possible connection to teacher effectiveness. As in several of the other context areas, the differences among subject fields and the teaching strategies suited to a given subject have not been seriously researched or considered. Recent major research efforts such as BTES and the Texas Teacher Effectiveness Study dealt primarily with elementary classes and focused on beginning classes in reading and English. Because of these major studies and possibly because of personal preference, many researchers and experts in the field of education have promoted single styles as the optimum method. For example, Joyce (1982) has promoted coaching; Hunter (1984), structured lesson; Taba (1962), induction; Bayles (1960), inquiry; Stallings (1980), directed teaching for remedial work; and Brophy and Evertson (1974), directed teaching for remedials and low SES.

Oversimplification admittedly does injustice to the fine work of these researchers and theorists. Nevertheless, one of the resultant impressions in the field is that BTES encourages developing the skills of directive teaching. Smith (1983), writing in reaction to recent research in teaching effectiveness (including BTES), stated it was true that "direct instruction is based on generalizations that do not hold for every member of a class. There can be little doubt that aptitude-treatment variation is a fact, but the number of variables involved is so overwhelming that useful results of research may not be obtained in the foreseeable future." (489–90) He further suggested that a "large proportion of students will always profit from direct instruction and the more we learn about effective performance in this mode, the better." (490) Yet in the same article Smith stated, "The performance of teachers is shaped by many variables and . . . among these is the content of instruction. . . . In the teaching of concepts, for example, the way teachers and students interact will be considerably different from the way they interact when skills are being taught." (491)

Peterson and Walberg (1979), Brophy and Good (1974), and Medley (1977) tend to agree that the effectiveness of the approach depends upon the type of student. For example, beginning students, low SES students in primary grades, and remedial students work best with direct approaches; high SES students and those in the intermediate level through high school work well with both direct and open approaches. However, what is not considered in their studies is the special requirements of the various disciplines as students progress through the grades. As Smith (1983) stated, a subject such as English literature that is heavy in concepts must be approached differently from a class such as physical education that is heavy in skills. To compound the issue further, English at the intermediate and secondary levels is a particular problem, for it includes, according to the organic field model, the skills of reading and writing, the content (substance) of literature, language study, and rhetoric, and the processes of cognition and creative thinking.

Recent studies of curricular structure (Walberg, Steele, and House 1974; Kuert 1979) have classified student perceptions of the nature of the work required in four secondary subject areas: language arts, mathematics, science, and social studies. Walberg and associates found that language arts deals with the cognitive operations of interpretation, evaluation, synthesis, and translation, as well as with the affective processes of student independence and participation in discussion. The consideration of alternative answers or creation of new ones is also a factor. These would be classified under the process variable of the organic field model. Because of these factors, language arts was seen as divergent in the study.

Mathematics, on the other hand, deals with analysis and memory, along with the affective conditions of test and grade stress, the absence of humor, and little discussion. The perceived objective was the "right answer"; hence, mathematics was seen as convergent. These results represent student perceptions and should not be taken as statements of the actual dimensions of English and math. However, the possibility of differences among the curricular structures of these subjects remains very strong. Also important to consider are the changes that take place as the student grows from novice to expert within a discipline. Both dimensions—subject differences and ability differences—may require several different styles of teaching for optimum growth.

The danger is that earnest and well-meaning educators and legislators will conclude that the current research on teacher effectiveness, with its firm message of teacher-directed methods for low SES beginners and remedial students in reading and mathematics, applies to all subjects, all levels, and all students. We need to identify where these teaching styles are optimal: directed teaching, presentational (lecture, demonstration), supervisory, coaching, inquiry (inductive, probing, discovery), and managerial (*Foxfire*, productions, internships). In English specifically, we need to become proficient in all styles throughout a professional career.

Text Materials and Curriculum

The area of text materials and curriculum as related to teacher effectiveness has not been adequately researched, perhaps because of the extreme difficulty in separating the variables. However, the probability that materials and curriculum have an effect appears to be quite strong. For example, Rosenshine (1971) reported on Pidgeon's 1970 study of arithmetic achievement, comparing 3,000 ten- and eleven-year-old students in California with 3,000 students of the same age in England. The results were dramatic. A thousand English students scored above 38 on a seventy-item test, while only fifty-three California students scored above 38. The major difference was in the curriculum. All of the material had appeared one to two grades earlier in the English textbooks than it did in the California texts. Even if the California teachers had high expectations for their students, those positive attitudes could not have overcome a deficient text and course of study.

The results in reading and literature for the National Assessment of Educational Progress 1979–80 are particularly telling for the teaching of secondary school English. The response patterns of thirteen- and seventeen-year-olds were similar except that the younger students were far more likely to make evaluative statements about what they read. The older students provided more evidence for their assertions, but they did not seem to possess strategies for examining a text, and their explanations were superficial and limited. They had not learned by age seventeen how to look for evidence for their judgments. Consequently, the researchers urged a major restructuring of curriculum in English classes to correct the problem. In particular, they suggested that more situations must be created that require students to explain and defend their opinions at length. This technique would correspond to the fusion of variables in the organic field model in that this kind of activity would require the interaction of skills, processes, and substance. The NAEP results also suggest that the emphasis on basic skills in the 1970s as the model for English may have contributed to the low performance of the seventeen-year-olds. Furthermore, we wonder how much the intellectual development of our students is affected by the current move to centralize, politicize, and consequently purge literature texts of controversial material, especially material written by minorities. It seems evident that curriculum design is a powerful variable on teaching effectiveness in English.

The Larger Profession

Throughout this discussion, the questions appear to be far more numerous than the answers. The organic field model suggests that the larger profession of the English teacher acts as a context, and this indeed may be the case for some teachers. The leadership provided by the larger profession does have some impact on the teaching practices of the rank-and-file teacher, but the verifiable proof is slim and somewhat discouraging. Change in educational practice is extremely slow, and even if it is carried out widely for a while, it may drop out of vogue after the original enthusiasm from the promoters has disappeared. Even at best, it probably takes ten years for an idea to be accepted and practiced by a significant number of teachers.

We suggest that the problem might lie in the inherent difficulty of the profession to gain a clear idea of the structure of English education. Lack of definition in turn encourages a piecemeal approach to the development of professional practice. Since the new idea or strategy is not assimilated into a total picture of the field, and since it may not appear at the onset to make a significant difference, the technique is dropped. Milner (1983) explores this difference between the practices advocated by the NCTE leadership and the actual practices of the rank-and-file English teacher. They found major differences, in that an idea strongly advocated by the leadership is usually *not* practiced by English teachers.

Far stronger for most teachers are the beliefs and practices maintained by informal and formal tradition, very often strengthened by publishers and encouraged by administrators and parents. Many of these practices may be common-sense axioms of effective teaching, but some are basically mythical ideas directly contraindicated by the best professional judgment and research. For example, the technique of using grammar study as a means for improving composition has been refuted by more than fifty years of research (Braddock, Lloyd-Jones, and Schoer 1963; Elley et al. 1976). More recently Hillocks (1984), in a meta-analysis of experimental treatment studies on composition, found that grammar actually has a negative effect on improving composition. The focus of instruction having the best effects was "inquiry," with "scales" second, "sentence combining" a close third, "models" fourth, and "free writing" fifth. All of these instructional practices showed positive effects, making them useful in the teaching of composition. On the other hand, grammar and mechanics were ineffective as foci of instruction. Hillocks comments,

> Taught in certain ways, grammar and mechanics instruction has a deleterious effect on student writing. In some studies a heavy emphasis on mechanics and usage (e.g., marking every error) results in significant losses in overall quality. School boards, administrators, and teachers who impose the systematic study of traditional school grammar on their students over lengthy periods of time in the name of teaching writing do them a gross disservice that should not be tolerated by anyone concerned with the effective teaching of good writing. Teachers concerned with teaching standard usage and typographical conventions should teach them in the context of real writing problems. (160)

Thus, even though researchers and professional leaders in the field of English reject the teaching of grammar in isolation as a strategy for writing improvement, tradition and public opinion directly support such practice. Because of this support, the most widely sold English textbook is a traditional grammar book. On an informal note, people tend to associate school English with grammar more than with any other aspect, and the association is generally negative.

English as a school subject does not have an official list of literary selections suitable for each grade level. Occasionally, as in recent actions by the California Superintendent of Schools, efforts are made to establish an official list, but unofficially the situation may be different. Literary selections are often made by teachers at certain grade levels, not because the selections are essential and appropriate or even useful in the curriculum, but merely because it has always been this way. Perhaps if more teachers were aware that publishers tend to call books "classics" if they remain on a list for twenty-five years, then curriculum committees could make more appropriate selections to help develop a nation of readers.

In their development of protocol materials in literature, Lid and Handler (1975) hypothesize that each reader creates a specific content for each piece of literature. The specific content would vary from that of another reader as a result of the particular experiences (individual context) of the reader. This study, along with others in the past decade of research in reader response, has opened our minds to the uniqueness of each reader. (See the work of Rosenblatt[1978], Purves and Rippere [1968], Bleich [1975], Holland [1968], and Squire [1964], to name a few.) We also know from countless reading-interests studies (among them, Purves and Beach 1972) the usual topics of greatest interest to our young readers. We are also aware of the need to develop bridges carefully to assist young readers in making the leap to the context of a difficult literary work. Yet the problem of inappropriate selections turning away many students persists, primarily because of the stranglehold of tradition, and partly because of the control that textbook publishers have over the English curricula in the United States.

Also critical are the traditional practices of teaching spelling, vocabulary, grammar, usage, reading comprehension, and the like as if they were completely separate subjects. Professional leadership recommends integrating these skills with literature and composition to provide a realistic reason for learning the skills. The organic field model discussed in chapter 1 describes the reason for this imperative of integration.

The profession of teaching English has seen exciting and fruitful developments in theory as a result of Project English, the Dartmouth Conference, NCTE journals and books, guidelines, conventions, and the writing projects. However, as long as rank-and-file teachers remain basically isolated from colleagues (Rosenholtz 1985), and as long as English teachers accept large classes and poor working conditions, the remonstrations from the larger profession to change ineffective practices will probably go largely unheard and unheeded. The problem is indeed difficult.

Summary and Implications

The research discussed in this section suggests that children generally exhibit different behaviors at different ages and levels of maturity, thus requiring various management and teaching styles. Positive feedback and direct teaching styles appear to be successful with young children, low SES groups, and remedial classes. Ability variance, which increases as students progress through school, becomes a difficult problem for secondary school teachers, especially in English. If the classes are extremely heterogeneous, the mode of teaching that the teacher selects may be inappropriate.

Differences apparently exist between junior high and high school students who are average and above-average. Studies on cognitive processes show apparent differences in the learning styles of weak and good problem-solvers, thus requiring completely different strategies for these groups. The research also points to differences between skills classes and concept courses. Math classes are perceived as primarily convergent, whereas English classes are perceived as primarily divergent, suggesting a need for appropriate and different teaching strategies. Researchers stress the need for all teachers to master direct teaching techniques and to use others as appropriate.

The careful selection of texts is essential, and misjudgments may have long-term deleterious effects on student achievement even with "good teaching." In English we must be vitally concerned with assignment practices and develop the skills to master direct and indirect teaching methods to be successful with children at various developmental and skill levels. Teacher transfers to English from other departments must be carefully considered, since the techniques for successful teaching are not the same from subject to subject. Time should be spent in retraining a reassigned teacher.

The expert opinion and findings of leading researchers in English education may be contrary to the actual practices that rank-and-file teachers use. In part, this situation may exist because most working teachers do not have time to read the professional journals and may not have the money to attend conferences. There is also strong evidence that teachers prefer to use teaching strategies sanctioned by tradition and local practice. Although English educators have developed much solid knowledge about effective teaching practices and curriculum content, the resistance against change, especially in English, outweighs the efforts of the leadership to move the profession towards significant improvement.

Conclusion: Context Variables and Teacher Effectiveness

In a recent article, Weaver (1985) discusses the work of some scientists (Capra, Prigogine, Stengers, Koestler, Zukav, Lakoff, and Johnson) in relation to the work of other researchers and theorists in English language arts (Rosenblatt, Iser, Holland, Bleich, and Fish in literature; Vygotsky in language; and Smith and Goodman in reading). She points out that the mechanistic metaphor and model has served in the recent past as a prism to view reality, and by that means we have been able to "understand, predict and control our world." (314) But recent paradigms in science are characterized by organicism rather than by mechanism. Weaver suggests that this organic paradigm, which appears to be developing in science and English studies, must "somehow transcend the simplistic dichotomy I have been describing and demonstrate the ways in which both mechanism and organicism are simultaneously true." (314) In summarizing the parallels found between the theorists in science and those in English, she says that they both "share an emphasis on organicism and process, specifically the process of transaction between interdependent entities." (312)

In a similar vein, the organic field model of the teaching of English focuses holistically on the interaction of substance, process, skills, and context as the essence of English teaching. This is presented as a model for English as it is taught in the schools. Although the context variable has not been explored frequently by researchers in either English or general education, the selected studies examined in this description point to the pervasiveness and power of the context variable to shape the course of English education. Although there may be no effective solutions to problems involving many of the context subvariables, there is certainly value in simply bringing the conditions and definitions of context to awareness. As long as context remains in the background, it goes unnoticed and consequently ignored, even though its effects dramatically shape what happens in the English classroom.

The organic field model serves to bring the heretofore invisible context into relief so that the relationships among all the variables of English can be seen. It is true that the effects—both positive and negative—of context are not easily discoverable. Now that these have been considered, it seems reasonable to conclude that, in order to examine whole environments such as teaching, educational research might be accomplished better by ethnographic techniques than by empirical research. The interaction of context with the other variables of English is thus a vital and central subject for research. The more we learn about this interaction and how to create more effective teaching techniques, the more successful will be our efforts to educate all children.

The New Teacher and Context

An abstract discussion of a model using findings from research and informed opinion may be supportive in working through the relationships of that model, but applying it directly to actual working situations is also useful. To this end, a case study of the context of a new teacher is presented here. Although the study is a composite of several new teachers, the situations are true. Because space does not permit, only some of the context variables and their probable effects are described.

Case Study

Ms. N. T. is thirty-two years of age, divorced, and the mother of two primary school children. She majored in communications studies at a midwestern state university and graduated with a 3.5 grade point average. Following her graduation from college, she worked as a television news reporter, a newspaper reporter, and a magazine editor. When she applied to a teacher preparation program at a state university, her application was denied because an admissions policy required English teacher trainees to have a major in English. She then applied to a large city school district for a position and was hired to teach English in junior high school on an emergency credential. Finally, she reapplied to the university for a special training program for emergency hires and was accepted.

Because of tax policies in this state, school funds were limited, slowing teacher raises and increasing the number of students in classes. This tax law, together with an extraordinary increase in immigrants from Asia, Mexico, and South America and an unusually heavy retirement rate of veteran teachers, put the school district in a state of extreme emergency. Teacher dissatisfaction was high and student performance was low.

Another legislative action allowed the district to establish a credential training program for untrained teachers who were hired on emergency credentials. The training program extended over a two-year period. If the trainees met the conditions of regular attendance at training sessions and successful teaching service, they would receive a regular teaching credential. Also, the pay for entering teachers was raised to about $20,000 per year, thus providing a more competitive salary for beginning teachers.

As part of the special program for trainees, Ms. N. T. was given the option of studying for her master's degree, which meant that she would take advanced courses at the university in place of the district workshops. Ms. N. T. was assigned to teach journalism, yearbook, seventh grade English, and eighth grade English. She had three classrooms and no books for the classes except for a class set of dictionaries and literature anthologies published in the early 1960s.

Other than the yearbook class, her classes contained thirty to thirty-seven students, primarily Hispanic and some recently arrived Asian students. The school is in a low SES community where both parents have to work or are on welfare. Her journalism class, being an elective, was filled with students who needed a class to fill out a program rather than with students who self-selected journalism because of their talent or interest in newspapers or writing.

Because of her inexperience and lack of formal teacher training before taking the teaching position, Ms. N. T. had to manage her new classes while attending the university in the evening. In addition, as a new teacher she was required to attend orientation meetings after school about once a week. She also had to take care of her two children.

As a matter of policy, the school district gives only half pay for September because school does not officially begin until the middle of September. No remuneration was provided for the three-week presemester training program that Ms. N. T. was required to take, even though she had to attend the entire day every day during the workshop. Because of the financial difficulties arising from these district policies, she chose to live with her parents in a small town in an adjoining county. The daily drive to work took about one hour each way. She had to arise at 5:00 A.M. to prepare her children for their school and to arrive at her own school by 7:30 A.M. Although she was supposed to have a preparation period the second hour of the school day, she was called to substitute regularly for absent or tardy teachers.

Ms. N. T.'s classrooms were scattered throughout the campus. She shared rooms with a math teacher, a social studies teacher, and another new English teacher. Because of the cutbacks in maintenance, her classrooms were swept only once a week. Most of the grounds around the buildings were unplanted and dusty. One of the classrooms was next to the physical education area. Since the September and October afternoons in southern California are often unbearably hot, she had to leave the windows open. The noise from the P.E. classes and band practice easily distracted her students.

Although her classes had large enrollments, only about half of her students attended on any given day. She could not plan for any continuing activity or project requiring that certain students be in attendance. On one occasion, she had assigned parts for a play in advance and had set up rehearsals for the presentation, but on the day of the performance only one of her major characters showed up. In December she found that many of her students had taken the entire month as a Christmas vacation to visit relatives in Mexico.

Although Ms. N. T. enjoyed teaching the creative and interesting lessons given to her by her methods instructor and other veteran teachers in her school, she found herself relying on a set schedule for her English classes with almost no composition work, simply because she had no time to correct the papers. Her spelling lessons were based on lists for the seventh and eighth grades that the chair of her department provided. She used the vocabulary words and literature questions in the 1960 literature anthology and the exercises from a traditional grammar text issued for her classes. No texts were provided for the journalism or yearbook classes.

The students were frequently disruptive or inattentive. On several occasions, students fell asleep at their desks. Ms. N. T.'s repeated attempts to send disruptive students out of the room only resulted in their returning the next day without a serious reprimand and ready to begin their disruption all over again. By mid-November, she was complaining of severe headaches, nervousness, fatigue, and lack of sleep. She was seriously considering resigning from her job.

Ms. N. T. spent the Thanksgiving holiday with a bad case of the flu, but managed to return to her work until the mid-winter recess. She was ill during most of the holidays and was again making plans to resign. Her colleagues at the school and university encouraged her to stay. Her professors commented on her talent and her successes with the classes, despite all of the early problems. Her second semester proceeded much more smoothly.

She is now in her second year of teaching, and her attitude and effectiveness have improved markedly. She has taken classes in English methods, secondary curriculum, reading in secondary school, educational psychology for inner-city schools, field studies, supervised teaching, and teaching ESL and bilingual students. She has her own classroom and time to plan for her students and is able to deal adequately with their behavior and erratic attendance. She enlists the aid of her students in managing the classroom, including keeping it clean and attractive. She has attended several local English conferences, both as a participant and as a speaker.

Ms. N. T. complains about colleagues who cannot control their students and who do not seem to know what to teach. And of course there are still the problems of teenage pregnancies, alcoholism, drug addiction, gang activity, and poverty.

Discussion

Although this seems like an unusual case, unfortunately the pattern is repeated over and over each fall in many major cities. In this case, the teacher was able to struggle through the difficulties of the first semester. Because of Ms. N. T.'s intelligence, determination, and strong support from colleagues and teachers, her experience turned into a success story. Much of her success lay in her ability to deal with her teaching environment. The following is an outline of the contextual problems:

First: Ms. N. T. had no knowledge of the world of her students. She was unaware of their educational needs and knew nothing of their cultural patterns. She reverted to what she remembered to be English (traditional grammar) and used methods she remembered from her own childhood (assigning chapters in textbooks and the questions at the end of the chapter). She blamed her students for their failure to learn.

Second: Her lack of training and subject matter background made it impossible for her to make independent decisions about the curriculum specific to her students. Also, because of her full schedule outside of school, she lacked the time to do the requisite planning. She therefore relied on outdated and inappropriate textbooks.

Third: The policy of the school and the district was responsible for hiring her on an emergency basis and contributed to her sense of failure in the first months by not being able to support her in ways that she needed. The discipline policies at the school made conducting her classes difficult. And the budget problems in the district made it difficult for her to work in relatively clean surroundings. Her working conditions were worsened because she had no classroom of her own and thus no opportunity to establish her own educational environment. Because of budget restrictions on films and other audiovisual materials, she was unable to enrich her classes with special materials.

Despite these problems, Ms. N. T. did have one crucial contextual asset: she was in a program where other beginning teachers were dealing with similar problems and where she received regular training from her school and university during the critical first year. She therefore developed a more positive attitude towards her students and her job.

The effects of the contextual variables for this new teacher were nearly disastrous, producing high stress in an almost hostile environment at the beginning of her career. As Ms. N. T. learned effective techniques for dealing with her students, the subject matter, and the context of her teaching, she became a successful teacher.

This abbreviated case study may be all too familiar to many English teachers. The basic argument is that, as English educators charged with the responsibility of training teachers, we must enlarge our view of the job of English teachers. It is not enough to teach them how to teach *Huckleberry Finn* to willing students. We must teach our beginning teachers how to be effective within the context of their teaching environments and how to work within that context to teach an interrelated English program.

References

Allington, R. March 1978. Are Good and Poor Readers Taught Differently? Is That Why Poor Readers are Poor Readers? Paper presented at the annual meeting of the American Educational Research Association, Toronto. ED 153 192.

Applebee, A. N. 1974. *Tradition and Reform in the Teaching of English: A History.* Urbana, Ill.: National Council of Teachers of English.

_____ . 1977. *A Survey of Teaching Conditions in English.* Urbana, Ill.: ERIC/ RCS and the National Council of Teachers of English. ED 151 796.

Armstrong, D. G. April 1983. Evaluating Teacher Induction Processes Associated with the Conditions of Practice. Paper presented at the National Council of Teachers of English Spring Convention, Seattle. ED 231 799.

Bayles, E. 1960. *Democratic Educational Theory.* New York: Harper and Brothers.

Berliner, D. C. April 1977. *Instructional Time in Research on Teaching.* Far West Laboratory for Educational Research and Development.

Berliner, D. C., and B. Rosenshine. 1976. *The Acquisition of Knowledge in the Classroom* (Beginning Teacher Evaluation Study Technical Report IV-1). Far West Laboratory for Educational Research and Development. ED 146 158.

Bleich, D. 1975. Readings and Feelings: An Introduction to Subjective Criticism. Urbana, Ill.: National Council of Teachers of English.

Bolster, A. S., Jr. 1983. Toward a More Effective Model of Research on Teaching. *Harvard Educational Review* 53:294–308.

Braddock, R., R. Lloyd-Jones, and L. Schoer. 1963. *Research in Written Composition.* Champaign, Ill.: National Council of Teachers of English. ED 003 374.

Brookover, W. B., C. Beady, P. Flood, J. Schweitzer, and J. Wisenbaker. 1979. *School Social Systems and Student Achievement: Schools Can Make a Difference.* New York: Praeger.

Brophy, J. E. 1983. Classroom Organization and Management. *The Elementary School Journal* 83:265–85.

Brophy, J. E., and C. M. Evertson. 1974. *Process-product Correlations in the Texas Teacher Effectiveness Study* (Report No. 74-4). Austin: The Univ. of Texas at Austin, Research and Development Center for Teacher Education.

Brophy, J. E., and T. L. Good. 1974. *Teacher-Student Relationships: Causes and Consequences.* New York: Holt, Rinehart and Winston, Inc.

Chanan, G., ed. 1973. *Towards a Science of Teaching.* Windsor, Berkshire: NFER Publishing Co., Ltd.

Chichon, D. J., and R. H. Koff. March 1978. The Teaching Events Stress Inventory. Paper presented at the annual meeting of the American Educational Research Association, Toronto. ED 160 662.

Conrad, K. J., and J. Eash. 1983. Measuring Implementation and Multiple Outcomes in a Child-Parent Center Compensatory Education Program. *American Educational Research Journal* 20:221–36.

Cooper, H. M., and T. L. Good. 1983. *Pygmalion Grows Up.* New York: Longman.

Davis, J. 1979. *Dealing with Censorship.* Urbana, Ill.: National Council of Teachers of English.

Denham, C., and A. Lieberman, eds. 1980. *Time to Learn: A Review of the Beginning Teacher Evaluation Study.* Washington, D.C.: The National Institute of Education. ED 192 454.

Duckworth, K., E. Kehoe, W. DeBevoise, and F. Donovan. 1981. *Creating Conditions for Effective Teaching.* Eugene: The Univ. of Oregon Center for Educational Policy and Management. ED 209 771.

Dunkin, M. J., and B. Biddle. 1974. *The Study of Teaching.* New York: Holt, Rinehart and Winston.

Dusel, W. J. 1955. Determining an Efficient Teaching Load in English. *Illinois English Bulletin* 43:1–19.

Education Commission of the States. 1981. *Reading, Thinking and Writing: Results from the 1979-80 National Assessment of Reading and Literature.* Denver: National Assessment of Educational Progress.

Ellett, C., and H. Walberg. 1979. Principals' Competency, Environment, and Outcomes. In *Educational Environments and Effects,* ed. H. Walberg, 140-64. Berkeley, Calif.: McCutchan Publishing Co.

Elley, W. B., I. H. Barham, H. Lamb, and M. Wyllie. 1985. The Role of Grammar in a Secondary School English Curriculum. *New Zealand Journal of Educational Studies* 10 (1): 26–42. (Reprinted in *Research in the Teaching of English* 10 [1976]: 5–21.) ED 112 410.

Eubanks, E. E., and D. Levine. 1983. A First Look at Effective School Projects in New York City and Milwaukee. *Phi Delta Kappan* 64:697–702.

Evertson, C. M., J. P. Sanford and E. T. Emmer. 1981. Effects of Class Heterogeneity in Junior High School. *American Educational Research Journal* 18:219–32.

Fantini, M. 1982. Community. In *Improving Educational Standards and Productivity,* ed. H. Walberg, 313–40. Berkeley, Calif.: McCutchan Publishing Company.

Fenstermacher, G. D. 1983. How Should Implications of Research on Teaching Be Used? *The Elementary School Journal* 83:496–99.

Fetler, M. March 1982. Television Viewing and School Achievement. Paper presented at the annual meeting of the American Educational Research Association, New York.

Filby, N. N., and L. S. Cahen. 1978. *Teaching Behavior and Academic Learning Time in the B-C Period* (Beginning Teacher Evaluation Study Technical Note V-2b). San Francisco: Far West Regional Laboratory for Educational Research and Development.

Filby, N. N., R. Marliave, and C. W. Fisher. 1977. Allocated and Engaged Time in Different Content Areas of Second and Fifth Grade Reading and Mathematics Curriculum. New York. Paper presented at the annual meeting of the American Educational Research Association. ED 137 315.

Fisher, C. W., D. C. Berliner, N. N. Filby, R. Marliave, L. S. Cahen, and M. M. Dishaw. 1980. Teaching Behaviors, Academic Learning Time, and Student Achievement: An Overview. In *Time to Learn,* ed. C. Denham and A. Lieberman, 7–32. Washington, D.C.: Department of Education.

Fisher, C. W., N. N. Filby, and R. Marliave. 1977. Instructional Time and Student Achievement in Second Grade Reading and Mathematics. Paper presented at the annual meeting of the American Educational Research Association, New York. ED 137 293.

Frank, B. M. 1984. Effects of Field Independence-Dependence and Study Technique on Learning from a Lecture. *American Educational Research Journal* 21:669–78.

Fredrick, W. C., H. J. Walberg, and S. P. Rasher. 1980. Time, Teacher Comments, and Achievement in Urban High Schools. *The Journal of Educational Research* 73:63–65.

Gage, N. L. 1978a. *The Scientific Basis of the Art of Teaching.* New York: Teachers College Press.

———. 1978b. The Yield of Research on Teaching. *Phi Delta Kappan* 60:229–35.

———. 1983. When Does Research on Teaching Yield Implications for Practice? *The Elementary School Journal* 83:492–96.

Glass, G. V., and M. L. Smith. 1978. *Meta-analysis of Research on the Relationship of Class Size and Achievement.* Report No. OB-NIE-G-78-0103. San Francisco: Far West Laboratory for Educational Research and Development.

Golladay, M. A., and J. Noell, eds. 1978. *The Condition of Education: Statistical Report.* Washington, D.C.: National Center for Educational Statistics. ED 155 811.

Good, T. L., and J. E. Brophy. 1973. *Looking in Classrooms.* New York: Harper and Row.

Haertel, G. D., H. J. Walberg, L. Junker, and E. T. Pascarella. 1981. Early Adolescent Sex Differences in Science Learning: Evidence from the National Assessment of Educational Progress. *American Educational Research Journal* 18:329–41.

Hallinan, M. T., and A. B. Sorensen. 1985. Class Size, Ability Group Size, and Student Achievement. *American Journal of Education* 94:71–89.

Hannafin, M. J. 1983. Fruits and Fallacies of Instructional Systems: Effects of an Instructional Systems Approach on the Concept Attainment of Anglo and Hispanic Students. *American Educational Research Journal* 20:237–49.

Hargrove, E. C., S. G. Graham, L. E. Ward, V. Abernathy, J. Cunningham, and W. K. Vaughn. 1981. *Regulations and Schools: The Implementation of Equal Education for Handicapped Children.* Nashville, Tenn.: Institute for Public Policy Studies, Vanderbilt University.

Harris, A. J., C. Morrison, B. L. Serwer, and L. Gold. 1968. *A Continuation of the CRAFT Project: Comparing Reading Approaches with Disadvantaged Urban Negro Children in the Primary Grades.* U.S. Office of Education Project No. 5-0570-2-12-1. New York: Division of Teacher Education, City University of New York. ED 010 297.

Hedges, L. V., and W. Stock. 1983. The Effects of Class Size: An Examination of Rival Hypotheses. *American Educational Research Journal* 20:63–85.

Henry, G. H. 1984. Council and Conference: An Interpretation. *English Education* 16:226–37.

Herrington, A. J. 1985. Writing in Academic Settings: A Study of the Contexts for Writing in Two College Chemical Engineering Courses. *Research in the Teaching of English* 19:331–61.

Hillocks, G., Jr. 1984. What Works in Teaching Composition: A Meta-Analysis of Experimental Treatment Studies. *American Journal of Education* 93 (1): 133–70.

———. October 1985. Presentation at the UCLA/LA County Seminar on Primary Traits. Pacifica Hotel, Inglewood, Calif.

Holland, N. 1968. *The Dynamics of Reader Response.* New York: Oxford University Press.

Hunt, R. A. 1982. Toward a Process-Intervention Model in Literature Teaching. *College English* 44:345–57.

Hunter, M. 1984. Knowing, Teaching and Supervising. In *Using What We Know About Teaching,* ed. P. Hosford, 169–92. Alexandria, Va.: Association for Supervision and Curriculum Development.

Jenkins, W. 1977. Changing Patterns in Teacher Education. In *The Teaching of English: NSSE Seventy-sixth Yearbook,* Part 1, 260–81. Chicago, Ill.: NSSE.

Johnson, D., and L. Johnson. 1978. *Learning Disabilities: What Research Says to the Teacher.* Washington, D.C.: National Education Association.

Joyce, B., and B. Showers. 1982. The Coaching of Teaching. *Educational Leadership* 40 (1): 4–10.

Kahn, R. L., D. M. Wolfe, R. P. Quinn, J. D. Snoek, and R. A. Rosenthal. 1964. *Organizational Stress: Studies in Role Conflict and Role Ambiguity.* New York: John Wiley & Sons.

King, M. L. 1978. Research in Composition: A Need for Theory. *Research in the Teaching of English* 12:193–202.

Kohut, S., Jr. 1976. *The Middle School: A Bridge between Elementary and Secondary Schools.* Washington, D.C.: National Education Association.

Kryiacou, D., and J. Sutcliffe. 1977. Teacher Stress: A Review. *Educational Research* 29:299–306.

Kuert, W. 1979. Curricular Structure. In *Educational Environments and Effects,* ed. H. Walberg, 180–99. Berkeley, Calif.: McCutchan Publishing Co.

Kulik, C. C., and J. A. Kulik. 1982. Effects of Ability Grouping on Secondary School Students: A Meta-analysis of Evaluation Findings. *American Educational Research Journal* 19:415–28.

Law, A. I. 1980. *Student Achievement in California Schools—1979–80 Annual Report. Sacramento: California State Department of Education.* ED 195 559.

Lid, R., et al. 1974. *Protocol Materials in Literature.* Tampa, Fla.: National Resource and Dissemination Center at the University of South Florida.

Lid, R., and P. Handler. 1975. *Protokollon: Guide to the Film Series: Responding to Literature.* Tampa, Fla.: National Resource and Dissemination Center, University of South Florida.

Little, J. W. 1982. Norms of Collegiality and Experimentation: Workplace Conditions of School Success. *American Educational Research Journal 19:325–40.*

Loree, N. R. 1965. *Problem Solving Techniques of Children in Grades Four through Nine* (Cooperative Research Project No. 2608). Washington, D.C.: U.S. Department of Health, Education, and Welfare.

Marjoribanks, K. 1979. Family Environments. In *Educational Environments and Effects,* ed. H. Walberg, 15–37. Berkeley, Calif: McCutchan Publishing Co.

McDonald, F. 1976. *Teachers Do Make A Difference.* Princeton, N.J.: Educational Testing Service.

McGuffey, C. W. 1982. Facilities. In *Improving Educational Standards and Productivity,* ed. H. Walberg, 237–80. Berkeley, Calif.: McCutchan Publishing Co.

Medley, D. M. 1977. *Teacher Competence and Teacher Effectiveness: A Review of Process-Product Research.* Washington, D.C.: American Association of Colleges of Teacher Education. ED 143 629.

————. 1982. *Teacher Competency Testing and the Teacher Educator.* Bureau of Educational Research, School of Education, Report 2-4. Charlottesville, Va.: University of Virginia

Meyer, L. A., R. M. Gersten, and J. Gutkin. 1983. Direct Instruction: A Project Follow Through Success Story in an Inner-City School. *The Elementary School Journal* 84:241–52.

Milner, J. O. 1983. Towers and Trenches: Polar Perceptions of the English Curriculum. *English Education* 15:31–35.

Mishler, E. G. 1979. Meaning in Context: Is There Any Other Kind? *Harvard Educational Review* 49:1–19.

Natriello, G., and S. M. Dornbusch. 1983. Bringing Behavior Back In: The Effects of Student Characteristics and Behavior on the Classroom Behavior of Teachers. *American Educational Research Journal* 20:29–43.

Noli, P. 1980. A Principal Implements BTES. In *Time to Learn,* ed. A. Lieberman and C. Denham, 213–21. Washington, D.C.: National Institute of Education. ED 192 454.

O'Dea, P., ed. September 1985. Teachers Often "Misassigned" to Teach Reading, English. *Council-Grams* XLVIII (1): 3.

Odell, L., C. R. Cooper, and C. Courts. 1978. Discourse Theory: Implications for Research in Composing. In *Research on Composing: Points of Departure,* ed. C. R. Cooper and L. Odell, 1–12. Urbana, Ill.: National Council of Teachers of English.

Ornstein, A. C., and D. U. Levine. 1981. Teacher Behavior Research: Overview and Outlook. *Phi Delta Kappan* 62:592–96.

Pallas, A. M., and K. L. Alexander. 1983. Sex Differences in Quantitative SAT Performance: New Evidence on the Differential Coursework Hypothesis. *American Educational Research Journal* 20:165–82.

Peterson, P. L., and H. J. Walberg. 1979. *Research on Teaching: Concepts, Findings, and Implications.* Berkeley, Calif.: McCutchan Publishing Co.

Pettegrew, L. S., and G. E. Wolf. 1982. Validating Measures of Teacher Stress. *American Educational Research Journal* 19:373–96.

Powell, M. 1978. Research on Teaching. *Educational Forum* 43:27–37.

Purkey, S. C., and M. Smith. 1983. Effective Schools: A Review. *The Elementary School Journal* 83:427–52.

Purves, A. C. 1984. The Paradox of Research in Language Education. *English Education* 16:3–13.

Purves, A. C., and R. Beach. 1972. *Literature and the Reader: Research in Response to Literature, Reading Interests, and the Teaching of Literature.* Urbana, Ill.: National Council of Teachers of English.

Purves, A. C., and V. Rippere. 1968. *Elements of Writing about a Literary Work: A Study of Response to Literature.* Urbana, Ill.: National Council of Teachers of English.

Ralph, J. H., and J. Fennessey. 1983. Science or Reform: Some Questions about the Effective Schools Model. *Phi Delta Kappan* 64:689–96.

Reid, M., L. Clunies-Ross, B. Goacher, and C. Vile. 1981. *Mixed Ability Teaching: Problems and Possibilities.* London: NFER-Nelson Publishing Co.

Robinson, V. 1985. *Making Do in the Classroom: A Report on the Misassignment of Teachers.* Washington, D.C.: American Federation of Teachers, Council for Basic Education. ED 263 108.

Rosenblatt, L. 1978. *The Reader, the Text, the Poem.* Carbondale, Ill.: Southern Illinois University Press.

Rosenholtz, S. J. 1985. Effective Schools: Interpreting the Evidence. *American Journal of Education* 93:352–88.

Rosenshine, B. V. 1971. *Teaching Behaviors and Student Achievement.* London: National Foundation for Educational Research.

————. 1978. Academic Engaged Time, Content Covered, and Direct Instruction. *Journal of Education* 160 (3): 38–66.

————. 1983. Teaching Functions in Instructional Programs. *The Elementary School Journal* 83:335–51.

Rosenshine, B., and D. Berliner. 1978. Academic Engaged Time. *British Journal of Teacher Education* 4:3–16.

Rosenthal, R., and L. Jacobson. 1968. *Pygmalion in the Classroom.* New York: Holt, Rinehart and Winston.

Rumberger, R. W. 1983. Dropping Out of High School: The Influence of Race, Sex, and Family Background. *American Educational Research Journal* 20:199–220.

Rutter, M., B. Maughan, P. Mortimore, J. Ouston, and A. Smith. 1979. *Fifteen Thousand Hours: Secondary Schools and Their Effects on Children.* Cambridge, Mass.: Harvard University Press.

Shapson, S. M., E. N. Wright, G. E. Eason, and J. Fitzgerald. 1980. An Experimental Study of the Effects of Class Size. *American Educational Research Journal* 17:141–52.

Silvernail, D. L. 1979. *Teaching Styles as Related to Student Achievement.* Washington, D.C.: National Educational Association.

Simpson, A. W., and M. T. Erickson. 1983. Teachers' Verbal and Nonverbal Communication Patterns as a Function of Teacher Race, Student Gender and Student Race. *American Educational Research Journal* 20:183–98.

Sirotnik, K. A. 1982. The Contextual Correlates of the Relative Expenditures of Classroom Time on Instruction and Behavior: An Exploratory Study of Secondary Schools and Classes. *American Educational Research Journal* 19:275–92.

Sizer, T. R. 1983. High School Reform: The Need for Engineering. *Phi Delta Kappan* 64:679–83.

Smith, B. O. 1983. Some Comments on Educational Research in the Twentieth Century. *The Elementary School Journal* 83:488-92.

Smith, B. O., M. Meux, J. Coombs, G. Nuthall, and R. Precians. 1967. *A Study of the Strategies of Teaching.* Urbana, Ill.: Bureau of Educational Research, College of Education, University of Illinois. ED 029 165.

Smith, M. L., and G. V. Glass. 1980. Meta-analysis of Research on Class Size and Its Relationship to Attitudes and Instruction. *American Educational Research Journal* 17:419–33.

Soar, R. S. 1973. *Follow-through Classroom Measurement and Pupil Growth, 1970–71.* Final Report. Gainesville, Fla.: Institute for Development of Human Resources.

Squire, J. 1964. *The Responses of Adolescents while Reading Four Short Stories.* Urbana, Ill.: National Council of Teachers of English.

Stallings, J. 1975. Implementation and Child Effects of Teaching Practices in Follow Through Classrooms. *Monographs of the Society for Research in Child Development 40 (7–8).*

————. 1978. *Follow-through Classroom Observation, 1972–73. Palo Alto, Calif.: Stanford Project on Teaching Practices.*

————. 1980. Allocated Academic Learning Time Revisited, or Beyond Time on Task. *Educational Researcher* 9 (11): 11–16.

Stallings, J., M. Needels, and N. Stayrook. 1979. *How to Change the Process of Teaching Basic Reading Skills in Secondary Schools.* Final Report to the National Institute of Education. Menlo Park, Calif.: SRI International.

Stockard, J., and J. W. Wood. 1984. The Myth of Female Underachievement: A Reexamination of Sex Differences in Academic Underachievement. *American Educational Research Journal* 21:825–38.

Stulac, J. 1982. Discussion [on Educational Staff and Students]. In *Improving Educational Standards and Productivity,* ed. H. Walberg, 124–32. Berkeley, Calif.: McCutchan Publishing Co.

Swick, K. J. 1980. *Disruptive Student Behavior in the Classroom.* Washington, D.C.: National Education Association.

Swick, K. J., and P. Hanley. 1980. *Stress and the Classroom Teacher.* Washington, D.C.: National Education Association.

Sykes, G. 1983. Teacher Preparation and the Teacher Workforce: Problems and Prospects for the 80s. *American Education* 19 (2): 23–30.

Taba, H. 1962. *Curriculum Development: Theory and Practice.* New York: Harcourt Brace & World.

Tikunoff, W. J., and B. A. Ward. 1983. Collaborative Research on Teaching. *The Elementary School Journal* 83:453–68.

Veldman, D. J., and J. P. Sanford. 1984. The Influence of Class Ability Level on Student Achievement and Classroom Behavior. *American Educational Research Journal* 21:629–44.

Walberg, H. J. 1967. Dimensions of Scientific Interests in Boys and Girls Studying Physics. *Science Education* 51 (2): 111–16.

Walberg, H. J., ed. 1979. *Educational Environments and Effects.* Berkeley, Calif.: McCutchan Publishing Co.

————. 1982. *Improving Educational Standards and Productivity: The Research Basis for Policy.* Berkeley, Calif.: McCutchan Publishing Co.

Walberg, H. J., R. E. Bole, and H. Waxman. 1977. *School Based Family Socialization.* Unpublished manuscript.

Walberg, H. J., and S. P. Rasher. 1979. Achievement in Fifty States. In *Educational Environment and Effects,* ed. H. Walberg, 353–68. Berkeley, Calif.: McCutchan Publishing Co.

Walberg, H. J., J. Steele, and E. House. 1974. Subject Areas and Cognitive Press. *Journal of Educational Psychology* 66:367–72.

Wang, M. C., and H. J. Walberg. 1983. Adaptive Instruction and Classroom Time. *American Educational Research Journal* 20:601–26.

Weaver, C. 1985. Parallels between New Paradigms in Science and in Reading and Literary Theories: An Essay Review. *Research in the Teaching of English* 19:298–316.

Weber, G. 1971. *Inner-City Children Can Be Taught to Read: Four Successful Schools.* Occasional Paper No. 18. Council for Basic Education. ED 057 125.

Williams, P. A., E. H. Haertel, G. D. Haertel, and H. J. Walberg. 1982. The Impact of Leisure-Time Television on School Learning: A Research Synthesis. *American Educational Research Journal* 19:19–50.

Wolf, R. 1979. Achievement in the United States. *In Educational Environments and Effects,* ed. H. Walberg, 313–30. Berkeley, Calif.: McCutchan Publishing Co.

IV Research on Teaching Products and Processes

Miles C. Olson
Department of Education
University of Colorado

Summarizing reviews of research on teaching, Doyle (1977) made the following observation: "Reviewers have concluded, with remarkable regularity, that few consistent relationships between teacher variables and effectiveness criteria can be established." (164) Similar comments have been made over the years. Unfortunately, our profession, colleagues in other disciplines, and the public have come to believe that research on teaching lacks a solid basis.

Yet few fields are so heavily studied. *Dissertation Abstracts* devotes many pages in each volume to education. More than 1,500 journals are addressed to the worldwide educational community, and many regularly report research findings. Still, the feeling persists that we know little that we can "take to the bank."

The huge number and mixed quality of studies are a major problem. Most research scientists studying problems of a similar nature either collaborate or keep in close contact with each other. In the model followed in scientific research, a few large, well-funded studies always build on the findings and procedures of previous work. Research centers (usually in universities, but sometimes in industry) generally focus on a few highly specialized areas rather than on the idiosyncratic interests of individual researchers.

Education follows quite a different model. Its researchers are spread throughout the world with few real concentrations of scholars. The universities attempt to be centers of research in the United States and most other countries; however, the research efforts even in these institutions are diffuse rather than targeted. By and large, educational research is an individual matter, not an institutional one. The result is a diffuse array of subjects and methods, and the effect is to make synthesis of research findings a very difficult job.

The organic field model of teaching posited in chapter 1 of this report presents both a design for teaching and a delineation of variables to be considered in research. The complexity of research in English teaching becomes clear when one examines the model. To be true to the typical experimental paradigm, one would have to control all variables except for the one being manipulated—a difficult task under any teaching circumstance, but particularly so in a situation so complex as the English classroom.

There is a further problem. Most scientific fields have clearly established indicators by which the success of their experiments can be measured. Education is not so fortunate. In education, we must assess both product and process. Further, this assessment is neither clearly defined nor easily performed.

Assessing Product Variables

It would be logical to assume the only truly relevant product of teaching to be student learning. Given this assumption, one might expect that any study of teaching behavior would consider as its only dependent variable the achievement of the learner. In the ideal situation, that surely would be the case. However, because paper-and-pencil tests are often inadequate indicators of the total learning sought by the teacher and the educational system, researchers must often look to other measures. As a result, teacher and student behaviors themselves are sometimes used as outcome measures in classroom research and, as such, are considered products. So, at least two broad classes of product variables must be considered in teaching: student performance on written tests and actual observations of behavior in the classroom. The matter of outcomes is further complicated by the fact that processes are sometimes more important outcomes than are products. Processes are difficult to observe and quantify into forms accessible through conventional, empirical-research paradigms.

Why, in this age of achievement testing and accountability, would a researcher not be content with the vast array of available paper-and-pencil tests that supposedly represent the products of teaching? There are several reasons:

1. Much of the learning posited by the model on which this report is based is not easily measured by paper-and-pencil tests. Certainly, learning is not easily measured by multiple-choice or true-false items. The organic field model expects learning to occur in three substantive areas, in four skill areas, and in three process areas. A measure that ignores any of these areas does not adequately measure the results of what the model calls English teaching.

2. Much of what is most important to learn is not fully integrated into a student's cognitive system or his or her behavior until months (sometimes years) after the occurrence of educational experiences designed to develop the desired outcome. Educators therefore often find it necessary to make inferences about relationships between classroom activities and long-term learning as they plan curriculum and teaching strategies. They can then seek out various kinds of classroom behaviors that have logical relationships to the ultimate desired learning outcomes and project future learning from the occurrence of those behaviors. The "product" of instruction thus becomes a set of behaviors that have logical extensions to desired future understanding and knowledge.

3. Naturalistic inquiry, presently in vogue in educational research, encourages us to look at the processes of the classroom as products. The behaviors of the participants in the teaching-learning process thus become data for analysis. While the systematic observation and analysis of classroom behavior reached its peak in the 1960s, naturalistic inquiry has opened that door again in the 1980s. The result may be an expanded understanding of the classroom as a social entity.

Types of Product Assessment

Generally, two types of assessment procedures are used in the schools: paper-and-pencil measures and situational observations of behavior.

Paper-and-Pencil Measures

Among paper-and-pencil measures are included standardized tests, teacher-made tests, writing samples, and questionnaires or rating scales.

Standardized Tests

Most school systems in the United States today require some form of standardized testing of their students. If they follow anything like the organic field model, these same school systems are apt to have curricula that are at variance with the things measured by those standardized examinations. Standardized achievement tests are characterized by the following:

1. They often reflect a kind of least common denominator, often focusing primarily on the lowest levels of learning and typically ignoring completely the affective and creative dimensions of the process variable.

2. They tend to be machine-scoreable, a characteristic one would expect, given the huge number of tests requiring scoring each year. The effect of this restriction is that the items are seldom, if ever, open-ended. Thus students are forced to choose from among alternatives presented by the test-maker rather than provide their own solutions, the result being an omission of the creative dimension.

3. They tend to be norm-referenced rather than criterion-referenced. Test-makers report the levels of success of a large reference group; the school system may then make judgments concerning their students by referring to the norm group. While such a comparison may be of general interest, it provides little specific information about relationships between local student achievement and curriculum or teaching.

4. Many standardized tests have a high reading level; thus they require a comparatively high level of literacy for a student to score high on any content field test. Reading is only one of the four skill dimensions given in the field model; emphasizing it excessively in testing seems inappropriate.

5. Standardized tests are not generally designed to be used as individual tests. In spite of that fact, individual reports showing a student's performance on various parts of a test battery are commonly filed in the permanent records of a school, with copies sent home for parent information. What is not generally appreciated in the educational community is the substantial measurement error of many of these tests. Some have standard errors of measurement sufficiently large that a single score may represent a range of as many as twenty percentile points. This is not a serious consideration when the tests are used for group comparison; it *is* a problem when they are used in individual cases.

Teacher-made Tests

Tests that the teacher constructs have the advantage of being written with both educational objectives and classroom context clearly in mind. They may also include a variety of items (often "essay" or "short answer") that enable students to respond in somewhat more creative ways than is true for standardized tests. However, teacher-made tests often suffer from problems of reliability, in that the items are prepared for a single administration and there is little possibility for systematic checking of those items before administering the test. Evaluating essay responses is also difficult: a scoring system that is appropriate for one class may be inappropriate for another. Thus, consistency in standards from one administration of an essay test to another is often a problem.

It would seem that using a teacher-made test to provide outcome data in research on teaching is ideal. Teachers would prepare instruments in the context of their personal applications of the curriculum and experience with the classroom context. These instruments would then be used to indicate level of learning and become criteria in determining how successful the techniques the teachers used were.

Such an application has real potential. However, when one tries to generalize broadly to teaching behavior (at least within the limits of classical research paradigms), it is helpful to have a common outcome variable that is employed in several similar studies. By their very nature, teacher-made tests are idiosyncratic, since they are a reflection of the individual teacher's sense of the curriculum and the classroom context.

Writing Samples

The use of writing samples to measure achievement in composition is becoming more common each year. Because a writing sample is a real representation of a skill taught in a composition class, several states are now lifting samples from all students in selected grades or from carefully drawn samples of students from all or some grades. A serious threat to their true validity, however, is their failure to consider the broad model for the teaching of English. Typical assignments ignore the total context of the English classroom and ask students to write about tennis shoes or other general, nonsubstantive topics.

Writing samples suffer from a number of problems. First, since most samples are taken during comparatively short periods of time (the typical time allotted to write seems to be under thirty minutes), the writer is seldom able to engage the processes normally used during writing. The impromptu assignment also does not provide time for significant thought, let alone research, before or during the draft. Most assignments also tend to limit the time available for revision; proofing is sometimes possible, but little time remains for significant alteration of the text itself.

The assignments themselves sometimes either promote or interfere with quality of response. For example, the Colorado State Writing Assessment program shows that students' writing was clearly better on certain topics than on others (Olson 1983). Readers felt that the student writers knew more about some topics than others and that they were also more interested in some than in others. The result seemed to be better writing where the knowledge base and interest level were highest.

Generalizing from one test to another is often a problem with writing-based assessments. Research establishing protocols for comparing scores from one writing to another has not yet reached a point where it is very helpful. Future efforts may provide ways in which comparisons may reliably be made across topics, but such comparisons are difficult at this time.

The cost of scoring tends to be a problem for those using student writing as an indication of an educational outcome. Even though experienced readers can read rapidly and make reliable judgments, both holistic and analytic, the process still takes time. And it requires a human being rather than a machine to do the scoring. Once one gets past the matter of human time (and the expense related thereto), the process becomes a good deal more attractive. However, the matter of cost is clearly an important consideration.

Reliability of scoring is not a serious problem, at least when adequate training is provided. One statewide and many district assessments have been conducted at the University of Colorado. Using a standard holistic scoring method, scorers have always achieved at least + .83 reliability; similar results have been obtained using analytic scales (Olson 1983).

Many individuals feel it unnecessary to conduct analytic scoring of student papers, particularly for mechanics, since the standardized test data generally available purport to measure that variable. However there is good reason to question the relationships between actual writing performance and scores on the mechanics portion of a standardized test. In a recent study, that issue was examined.

In a districtwide assessment of the writing skills of students in a Colorado school district at grades 3, 5, 7, 9, and 11, a holistic rating and several analytic scales were included for each grade level (see Olson 1984). The analytic scales were based on the district's curriculum. After the scoring was completed, a correlation between scores on the mechanics analytic scale and the students' scores on a standardized achievement test of language-mechanics-editing achievement was computed. Surprisingly, correlations of only + .30 to + .18 were found, with the highest at the third grade and the lowest at the eleventh grade. Feeling these correlations to be very low, since the two variables purport to measure the same thing, the research group decided to look at other correlations within the standardized objective instrument itself. Upon examining correlations between the language-mechanics-editing section of the standardized test and the test's own scale representing intelligence, the group found overall correlations of + .95 and above. The group concluded that the two tests represented a multidimensional measure of a gestalt, not closely related to the actual separate skills and knowledges it purported to measure.

The use of writing samples as indicators of achievement is *prima facie* valid for measuring achievement in English so long as the circumstances under which the samples are taken are similar to those in which students apply their skills under normal conditions and so long as the assignment (topics) relate to the content and processes taught in the English classroom. Both holistic and analytic scoring can provide helpful information that relates to the effectiveness of variables in the learning environment.

Questionnaires or Rating Scales

These instruments are sometimes used to assess students' perceptions of various educational experiences. Student rating of teachers is commonplace in colleges and universities. Student input as to the quality of materials and experiences is often gathered through the use of rating instruments at many levels. One must be careful in using them, however. Studies of the use of teacher rating instruments at the college level sometimes show student learning as being inversely correlated with teacher ratings, although this is by no means a universal finding. It seems that these instruments are measuring a gestalt that is somewhat different from and perhaps larger than student achievement.

The conditions under which these instruments are administered are unfortunately often related to the results. In other words, if an individual wishes a certain result from a survey, he or she can sometimes manipulate the situation to get that result from the respondents. The way an instrument is written can bias responses.

Situational Observations of Behavior

School supervisors have been observing social and educational situations systematically for some time. However, Anderson's work in the late 1930s launched the scientific coding and analysis of interactive instructional behavior (Anderson 1937). Bales systematized the coding process further in the late 1940s (Bales and Gerbrands 1948). The 1950s and 1960s saw considerable interest in systematic description and analysis of instructional settings. The massive *Mirrors for Behavior* (Simon and Boyer 1967) includes more than one hundred instruments that have been used as research tools in attempts to describe social and instructional interaction.

The typical coding system establishes a set of behaviors that the researcher intends to look for. More often than not, this catalogue of behaviors comes from the research literature surrounding the phenomenon the researcher is investigating. However, it can also result from extensive noninvasive, open observation of the classroom and factor analyses of the behaviors identified (see Flanders 1960).

Coders are then trained to identify the selected behaviors. Some systems include a time variable; others merely code the occurrence of the identified behaviors. Elaborate systems for combining and analyzing the results of the coding are often included by the system designers.

There are two basic emphases of the systems used to analyze and describe instructional settings. The first is a focus on the affective dimension of the classroom; the second is a focus on the cognitive dimension.

Affective Systems

These systems deal with the emotional climate of the classroom. They often describe how that climate is influenced by teacher behaviors, especially those by which the teacher reacts to the feelings, actions, and ideas of the students.

The best-known of the affective systems is Flanders's Interaction Analysis (Flanders 1960). It contains only ten categories and can be coded easily by a researcher sitting in the actual classroom setting. This system requires the observer to code a behavior every three seconds or whenever the behavior changes. Since the instrument has a time dimension, it is possible to determine, on analysis, the approximate amount of classroom time devoted to each behavior. Flanders's elaborate matrix system permits detailed analysis of classroom behavior. A thorough description of the analytic system used with the instrument may be found elsewhere (Flanders 1966) and should be studied by anyone using this system seriously.

Other systems for describing the affective climate of the classroom are also available. Flanders's is one of the simplest to use; however, others probe more deeply into some specific areas of classroom behavior, such as reinforcement strategies or disciplinary techniques.

Cognitive Systems

Nearly all cognitive systems deal with levels of cognition; some even take Bloom's taxonomy of the cognitive domain and incorporate it verbatim into their coding schemes. Most, however, incorporate at least three levels: data recall, data processing, and evaluation.

Data recall, of course, involves the lowest levels of cognition. It encompasses memorization; in most systems, it also includes "putting it in your own words." Data processing may be coded when the student is doing something with information already learned. For example, the student might break it down or combine it with other information to develop new insights. Evaluation usually includes both opinion and judgment. Many category systems make a good deal of the distinction between public and private criteria on which evaluative judgments are made.

Taba (1964) was one of the earliest and most influential classroom analysts to work in the cognitive arena (see Taba, Levine, and Elzey

1964). She strongly believed that the content being taught was inseparable from the teaching process. Her system was designed to help teachers lead students into higher levels of thinking and thus into higher levels of understanding of the subject matter. It was shaped around three major categories: source, thought levels, and functions. Taba's system requires the observer to code each occurrence of a categorized behavior.

Accepting the notion that the teaching process may be a product in itself is difficult for most teachers. However, the fact that certain activities are happening in a classroom may be as important to the success of a curriculum as the learnings that are immediately apparent as a result of classroom acts. Paper-and-pencil evidence of classroom accomplishment is routinely accepted; however, it is difficult to measure long-term learning through such measures. Often, the curriculum specialist might be well advised to consider observing classroom activities as a logical point of inference to use in projecting future long-term learning. The hundreds of existing well-researched instruments available to the classroom researcher provide an ample base from which to begin. None, however, adequately represents the complexity of the total instructional setting that confronts English teachers.

In summary, there appears to be no body of research on teaching *in the English classroom* that can be brought to bear to assist the English teacher in coping with the organic field model. The best one can do is look to the field of education in general for guidance. The remainder of this chapter investigates insights from classroom research in general, seeking to provide some insights into potentially promising practices for the teacher of English.

Assessing Process Variables through Meta-analysis

A problem that research synthesizers have had is the absence of a technique to use in evaluating and weighting studies as they attempt to make generalizations from bodies of research. Should all studies, regardless of method or quality, be weighted similarly? Should only studies that follow rigorous experimental procedures be included? With hundreds of studies, no common experimental procedure, and varying populations, one faces an exceedingly difficult problem in attempting a synthesis of research findings. Without some technique to aid the reviewer in summarizing and synthesizing studies, one falls back on intuition to draw conclusions from a body of data so large as to be beyond serious intuitive manipulation. If reviewers were to do a perfect job, they would have to analyze each study, going into the methodology, the nature of the populations and the treatments, and the database from which the findings emerged. Clearly, most reviewers have not done that, and even those who have (in certain quite narrow areas), have found a conceptual quagmire that is extremely difficult to understand.

In 1976, Glass, in his presidential address to the American Educational Research Association, detailed a process that has become an important aid in synthesizing research data from many studies. The technique, referred to as meta-analysis (Glass 1978), has become a primary tool in the synthesis and reanalysis of research data in education as well as in other fields. It permits the researcher to weigh the value of discrete pieces of data, join them, and synthesize the joined data. Interpretation and generalization then become reasonably straightforward and are databased rather than intuitive, as is the case in most common reviews.

Recent applications of meta-analysis techniques in education have revealed much interesting and useful information. While many areas of the field have been studied with this technique, this report focuses primarily on those studies that synthesize primary research on the teaching process. The reader should be aware that (1) these studies come from many grade levels and content areas, (2) outcome measures are often standardized measures that reflect only a part of the learning envisioned in the organic field model for English teaching, and (3) the studies that make up the databases for these meta-analyses seldom consider a teaching paradigm as complex as that depicted in the organic field model.

Table 1 presents selected findings from two meta-analyses that relate to cooperative learning models and their effects on student achievement. The two analyses taken together represent the synthesis of 150 research efforts. The conclusion one must draw from this report is that cooperative learning, a classroom organizational variable at least somewhat under the control of the teacher, is a positive factor in producing positive relationships among students and in enhancing substantive learning. Individualized approaches to learning are consistently less effective than are either cooperative or group-competitive classroom structures.

Table 2 reports three meta-analyses that relate specific teaching variables to student achievement. The studies suggest a positive impact of advance organizers, the purposeful use of questioning techniques, and the use of praise.

Table 3 relates a single meta-analysis of grouping practices. The data suggest an overall positive effect on both achievement and attitude for ability grouping.

Another study, summarizing the results of fifty-nine studies relating to the impact of class size on achievement (Smith and Glass 1980) showed a mean effect size of .49. Teachers should be aware of this significant

Table 1

Synthesis of Research on Classroom Organization:
Cooperative, Competitive, Group-Competitive, and Individualistic

Author	No. of Studies	Mean Correlation or Effect	Percent Positive	Variables
Johnson et al. (1981)	122	.00	54	Cooperative vs. group-competitive
		.78	76	Cooperative vs. competitive
		.37	68	Group-competitive vs. cooperative
		.76	83	Cooperative vs. individualistic
		.59	81	Group-competitive vs. individualistic
		.03	47	Competitive vs. individualistic
Slavin (1980)	28	—	81	Cooperative learning and curriculum-specific tests
		—	78	Cooperative learning and standardized tests
		—	95	Cooperative learning and race relations
		—	65	Cooperative learning and mutual concern

finding, since negotiations between teacher organizations and school administrations often involve considerations of class size.

Tables 4 through 7 report selected findings of a massive summary of research by Walberg, Shiller, and Haertel (1979). Since this study does not employ the meta-analysis technique but rather simply counts the number of positive outcomes, its conclusions are less reliable than those based on the more sophisticated technique that weights the studies according to specific criteria. However, the sheer number of studies

Table 2

Synthesis of Research on Selected Teaching Techniques

Author	No. of Studies	Mean Correlation or Effect	Percent Positive	Variables
Luiten, Ames, and Ackerson (1980)	135	.23	—	Effects of advance organizers on learning and retention. Effects larger on 20+ days retention, higher achievers.
Redfield and Rousseau (1981)	20	.73	—	Effects of higher- and lower-order cognitive questions.
Wilkinson (1980)	14	.08	63	Effects of praise on achievement. Slightly more effective for lower socioeconomic groups and in math.

Table 3

Synthesis of Research on Ability Grouping
and Its Effect on Achievement and Attitude

Author	No. of Studies	Mean Correlation or Effect	Percent Positive	Variables
Kulik (1981)	51		71	Achievement on final exam
	15		47	Self-concept
	8		88	Attitude toward subject matter
	11		73	Attitude toward school

Table 4

Selected Data from a Summary of Research in Teaching Processes
(Walberg, Shiller, and Haertel 1979)

Topic	No. of Results	Percent Positive
Student-led vs. instructor-led discussion on		
Achievement	10	100.0
Attitude	11	100.0
Factual vs. conceptual questions on achievement	4	100.0
Psychological incentives and engagement		
Teacher cues to student	10	100.0
Teacher reinforcement of student	16	87.5
Teacher engagement of class in lesson	6	100.0
Individual student engagement in lesson	15	100.0
Lecture vs. discussion on		
Achievement	16	68.0
Retention	7	100.0
Attitude	8	86.0
Student-centered vs. instructor-centered discussion on		
Achievement	7	57.1
Understanding	6	83.3
Attitude	22	100.0

Table 5

Selected Data from a Summary of Research on Specific Teaching Traits
(Walberg, Shiller, and Haertel 1979)

Topic	No. of Results	Percent Positive
Specific teaching traits on achievement		
Clarity	7	100.0
Flexibility	4	100.0
Enthusiasm	5	100.0
Task-orientation	7	85.7
Use of student ideas	8	87.5
Indirectness	6	83.3
Structuring	3	100.0
Sparing criticism	17	70.6

Table 6

Selected Data from a Summary of Research on the Structure of Schooling
(Walberg, Shiller, and Haertel 1979)

Topic	No. of Results	Percent Positive
Open vs. traditional education on		
Achievement	26	54.6
Creativity	12	100.0
Self-concept	17	88.2
Attitude toward school	25	92.0
Curiosity	6	100.0
Self-determination	7	85.7
Independence	19	94.7
Freedom from anxiety	8	37.5
Cooperation	6	100.0

Table 7

Selected Data from a Summary of a Decade of Research on External
Factors Affecting Achievement
(Walberg, Shiller, and Haertel 1979)

Topic	No. of Results	Percent Positive
Motivation and learning	232	97.0
Social class and learning	620	97.0
Home environment on		
Verbal achievement	30	100.0
Reading gains	6	100.0
Math achievement	22	100.0

considered makes a reasonably good case for accepting the data. (In this summary, studies reporting negative and no-significant-difference findings were separated from those reporting significant positive outcomes; thus, the "Percent Positive" column represents a reasonably select population of studies.)

Table 4 reports findings from studies relating very specifically to the teaching act—how the teacher conducts the activities of the classroom.

The data fail to support a number of commonly held beliefs about teaching. For example, lecture seems more effective than discussion on retention, achievement, and attitude; student-led discussions seem more effective than teacher-led discussions.

Table 5 reports relationships between specific teaching traits and achievement. The data support the importance of teacher enthusiasm and confident management in the classroom.

Table 6 relates to a phenomenon somewhat outside the teacher's sphere of influence, except (as in the case of class size) when it becomes a matter of establishing policy. In the studies cited, open education seems superior to traditional forms on many counts. Of course, the community context will often interfere with changing the nature of the school and its curricular structure.

Table 7 presents summaries of studies of three factors outside the control of the teacher: motivation, social class, and home environment. As noted earlier, these factors are strongly related to student achievement.

The data presented above reveal that research tells us a good deal more about teaching and its relation to learning (both cognitive and affective) than we have generally believed. Just as Smith and Glass (1980), in their meta-analysis on class size and achievement, contradict the popular belief that size of class has little or no effect on achievement, so these new syntheses of research on teaching practice give us evidence that what teachers do may have a substantial relationship to what and how children learn.

What, then, can one conclude from the synthesized and summarized data presented here? The following generalizations seem supported by the data:

1. Cooperative learning-teaching situations seem to improve student achievement and attitude; individually structured and competitive educational environments seem less effective.

2. When teachers use advance organizers, students seem to achieve at a higher level than when organizers are not used.

3. When teachers ask higher-order questions, they are apt to increase student learning at higher, but not necessarily lower, cognitive levels.

4. Praise affects achievement to some extent, but seems most effective with children from lower socioeconomic backgrounds, in the primary grades, and in mathematics.

5. Class size does make a difference in student achievement; the difference is in the direction common sense says it should be, that smaller classes tend to be associated with higher achievement. The major impact, however, is not reached until class size drops below

fifteen, when substantial increases in achievement result as class size continues to drop.

6. Ability grouping in the secondary school seems related to increased achievement and improved student attitude.

7. Student-led discussions seem positively related to improved achievement at some levels.

8. Teacher traits such as clarity, flexibility, enthusiasm, task orientation, use of student ideas, indirectness, structuring, and use of little or no negative criticism seem related to increases in student achievement.

9. So-called open education is positively related to student achievement (although not strongly), creativity, self-concept, attitude toward school, curiosity, self-determination, independence, and cooperation when compared with traditional school structures.

10. Questioning behaviors used by teachers seem to be related to students' retention of class material, especially when questions are focused at the target cognitive level (e.g., fact-based questions help students retain facts; inference questions help students make inferences).

11. Motivation, social class, and home environment, which are outside the control of the school and teacher, seem to have a profound influence on student achievement. Developmental level and intelligence also have substantial effects on achievement, as do student peer-group memberships.

Conclusion

So where do these findings leave the inquiry begun in this report? Perhaps these data destroy a few long-held convictions and reinforce others. One conviction that this presentation should destroy is that all of our studies in education add up to one big "no significant difference." There is a considerable body of knowledge about our profession, and most of the truly concrete knowledge comes from classroom-based research studies. However, one might naturally worry that the generalizations from that research may not be applied wholesale to the English classroom. Teachers of English need to be aware of this information; however, those same teachers should apply these findings to the classroom cautiously and with a high awareness of the total array of content and context variables that constrain their teaching activities.

The data presented here, together with those revealed through other meta-analyses (see, as an example, Hillocks 1986), provide a basis on which teachers and curriculum planners can build a set of assumptions about teaching that may be applied judiciously when they seem appropriate in the context of the organic field model of English teaching. The authors are confident that enough is known now about teaching in general and English teaching in particular to begin developing some heuristics that may serve as guides for general practice. Certain heuristics have become commonplace in composition teaching as outgrowths of the writing-process research of the past decade; the present state of knowledge may permit the same to happen in the area of English teaching.

References

Anderson, H. H. 1937. An Experimental Study of Dominative and Integrative Behavior in Children of Pre-School Age. *Journal of Social Psychology* 8:335–45.

Bales, R. F., and H. Gerbrands. 1948. The "Interaction Recorder": An Apparatus and Checklist for Sequential Content Analysis of Social Interaction. *Human Relations* 1:456–63.

Butcher, P. M. 1981. *An Experimental Investigation of the Effectiveness of a Value Claim Strategy Unit for Use in Teacher Education.* Sydney, Australia: Macquarie Univ.

Doyle, W. 1977. Paradigms for Research on Teacher Effectiveness. In *Review of Research in Education*, Vol. 5, ed. L. S. Shulman, 163–98. Itasca, Ill.: F. E. Peacock Publishers.

Flanders, N. A. 1960. *Teacher Influence, Pupil Attitudes and Achievement: Final Report.* CRP Monograph no. 12. Washington, D.C.: Government Printing Office.

————. 1966. *Interaction Analysis in the Classroom: A Manual for Observers.* Ann Arbor: Univ. of Michigan.

Glass, G. V. 1978. Integrating Findings: The Meta-analysis of Research. *Review of Research in Education*, Vol. 5, ed. L. S. Shulman, 351–79. Itasca, Ill.: F. E. Peacock Publishers.

Hillocks, G., Jr. 1986. *Research on Written Composition: New Directions for Teaching.* Urbana, Ill.: National Conference on Research in English and ERIC/RCS.

Johnson, D. W., G. Maruyama, R. Johnson, D. Nelson, and L. Skon. 1981. Effects of Cooperative, Competitive, and Individualistic Goal Structures on Achievement: A Meta-analysis. *Psychological Bulletin* 89:47–62.

Kulik, C. L. C. 1981. *Effects of Ability Grouping on Secondary School Students.* Paper presented at the annual meeting of the American Educational Research Association. ED 204 417.

Luiten, J., W. Ames, and G. Ackerson. 1980. A Meta-analysis of Advance Organizers on Learning and Retention. *American Educational Research Journal* 17:211–18.

Olson, M. C. 1983. Relationships between Analytic Ratings of Compositions and Writer Performance on Standardized Achievement Instruments. Paper presented to the Colorado Board of Education.

————————. 1984. Establishing and Implementing Colorado's Writing Assessment Program. *English Education* 16:208–19.

Openshaw, M. K., and F. R. Cyphert. 1966. *The Development of a Taxonomy for the Classification of Teacher Classroom Behavior.* Cooperative Research Project No. 2288. Columbus: The Ohio State Univ. Research Foundation.

Redfield, D. L., and E. W. Rousseau. 1981. A Meta-analysis of Experimental Research on Teacher Questioning Behavior. *Review of Educational Research* 51:237–45.

Simon, A., and E. G. Boyer. 1967. *Mirrors for Behavior.* Philadelphia: Research for Better Schools.

Slavin, R. E. 1980. Cooperative Learning. *Review of Educational Research* 50:315–42.

Smith, M. L., and G. V. Glass. 1980. Meta-analysis of Research on Class Size and its Relationship to Attitudes. *American Educational Research Journal* 17:419–33.

Taba, H., S. Levine, and F. F. Elzey. 1964. *Thinking in Elementary School Children.* San Francisco: San Francisco State College.

Walberg, H. J., D. Shiller, and G. D. Haertel. 1979. The Quiet Revolution in Educational Research. *Phi Delta Kappan* 61 (3): 179–82.

Wilkinson, S. S. 1980. *The Relationship of Teacher Praise and Student Achievement: A Meta-analysis.* Unpublished doctoral dissertation. Gainesville: Univ. of Florida.

V Teacher Effectiveness Research: Inferences for In-Service and Staff Development

Richard L. Hanzelka
Mississippi Bend Area Education Agency
Bettendorf, Iowa

The purpose of an in-service or staff development effort in any mode is to improve teacher effectiveness. The intervention strategy used is an attempt to extend the teacher training experiences and properties described by Dunkin and Biddle (1974) in their model for the study of classroom teaching. In chapter 2 of this monograph, Peters cites research by Ryans (1960) and summarizes the research as follows:

> Teachers with more successful patterns of classroom behavior tended to have strong interests in many areas, to prefer student-centered learning situations, to be independent, to have superior verbal intelligence, and to be willing to allow nondirective classroom procedures. Teachers with less successful behavior patterns tended to prefer teacher-directed learning situations, to value exactness, orderliness, and "practical" things, and to be less tolerant toward the expressed opinions of pupils. They were also more restrictive and critical in appraising the behavior and motives of other persons.

It is assumed that teachers in practice can be identified as "more successful" or "less successful." If that assumption is correct, in-service and staff development trainers are faced with the question of whether in-service training carries over to the classroom—that is, whether students have gained in some way from the teacher's new training. Perhaps more importantly, those trainers must then decide what strategies will change a less successful teacher into a more successful one. The Bay Area Writing Project, the State of Iowa Writing Project, the several sites of the National Writing Project, and a variety of other in-service projects have typically trained already successful teachers to become more successful.

Patton (1982) sheds important new light on the issue of training teachers to be more successful, or "improved." He suggests the need to consider "improvement" and "change" as separate categories:

Let me suggest that for staff development evaluations it may be important to separate the issue of improvement from the related, but quite different issue of impact or change. Improvement involves a judgment about whether or not a change is for better or worse. It is crucial throughout the evaluation process that empirical observations about program impact be kept separate from judgments about whether or not such impact constitutes improvement. . . .

Questions of right and wrong, better or worse, are not simple empirical questions. To formulate evaluation questions solely in such terms can sabotage an evaluation from the beginning. What, then, can one do? In my judgment the empirical question is not improvement but change. I suggest that we begin not with the question of whether or not teachers are "better," but whether or not they are different. Has the program been effective in changing teachers? Do they think differently? Can they do things now that they couldn't do before? Do they feel differently? Are different things occurring in teachers, in classrooms? These are empirical evaluation questions. Data from these evaluation questions can then be used to determine whether or not such changes and differences constitute progress or improvement.

This is not an esoteric, semantic distinction. Nor is it the beginning of a polemic on value-free social science. It is a practical suggestion for distinguishing between that which can be observed (by whatever methods) and that which cannot be observed. Failure to make that distinction can lead to serious misunderstanding throughout the evaluation process. (12–13)

What is it that can make teachers different as a result of in-service training? What is it that causes changed behavior? Information by itself is insufficient, and yet a majority of teacher in-service sessions focus on just that information-imparting mode. The focus on skills and substance (referred to in earlier pages of this monograph) at the expense of process so often leaves the impact of English language arts teaching in-service on the cutting-room floor, rather than in the repertoire of the teacher. In a very real sense, such skills and substance focused in-service are not in-service in English language arts if actual process learning by the teacher is not involved. Graves and Stuart (1985) in *Write from the Start* address the issue:

Our whole educational system ignores the teacher's need to keep learning. The idea receives much lip service through in-service education, but because of the way most sessions are conducted, the teachers don't leave with a sense of having learned. Worse, the format of the workshop suggests that the leader knows everything and the teachers don't. That is bad medicine even if the workshop leaders are right, and of course they aren't.

If anything, the revolution in teaching writing has taken off because teachers are finding something in it for themselves. Their writing changes, their reading changes, and, above all, when they listen, the children demonstrate all the ways in which they learn. Thus, teachers become acquainted with a broad repertoire of techniques that can help them, as well as the children, learn. (128)

If in-service training is to be an important force in English language arts, decisions about how it should be conducted must be based on considerations beyond the time available and the cost of the speaker. Concepts such as the integration of language arts must be a part of the teacher's own experience as a learner before they can become part of regular classroom procedures. It is a matter of making sure that teacher in-service training focuses on the needs of the present audience of teacher-learners, rather than just on the absent audience of students.

The Variables

In determining what issues should be addressed in in-service training, we can take a cue from the Dunkin and Biddle (1974) model of the study of teaching presented in chapter 2 (p. 28). Presage, context, process, and product variables should be considered in any learning situation (for children or for adult professionals): the effectiveness of the teacher in any situation has a great deal to do with what is learned.

Presage Variables

The presage variables apply as much to in-service presenters who set up learning situations for teachers of younger students (K–12) as they do for pre-service teachers. If the Dunkin and Biddle model is adapted with "presenter" as a replacement for "teacher" and with "teacher" as a replacement for "students," some interesting dimensions begin to emerge (Figure 1, next page).

We must ask questions about the in-service presenter's formative experiences, training experiences, and properties. Has the presenter ever taught younger students? Why did the presenter leave teaching younger students? What are the teaching skills of the in-service presenter? What intelligence, motivation, and personality traits does the in-service presenter possess? To what extent can any of those traits be changed or adapted for new audiences of learners?

Other presage variables are often ignored if the in-service presenter has a certain charisma or an appealing style of delivery. Naftulin, Ware, and Donnelly (1973) reported the results of a study of presage variables. The hypothesis tested in the study was that, given a sufficiently impressive lecture paradigm, an experienced group of educators taking part in a new learning situation would feel satisfied that they had learned despite

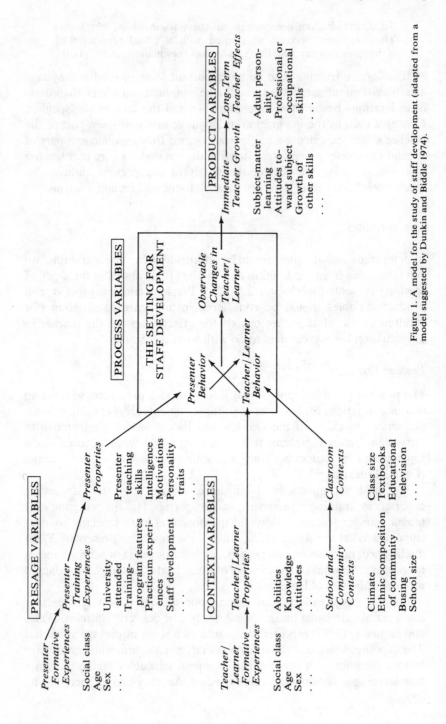

Figure 1. A model for the study of staff development (adapted from a model suggested by Dunkin and Biddle 1974).

irrelevant, conflicting, and meaningless content conveyed by the lecturer. To test the hypothesis, the authors asked a professional actor, who was given an impressive curriculum vitae, to lecture three groups of highly trained educators. The authors concluded that "the study serves as an example to educators that their effectiveness must be evaluated beyond the satisfaction with which students view them and raises the possibility of training actors to give 'legitimate' lectures as an innovative approach toward effective education." (630) They emphasized that student satisfaction with learning may be little more than an illusion of having learned.

The "properties" of the in-service presenter would appear to be as crucial as any of the variables involved in a typical in-service setting. In an in-service encounter of a day or less, a presenter may have personality traits and a certain charisma that overpower other factors, including lack of teaching skill. In an extended staff development course or workshop, teaching skills, experience in teaching, and a variety of other presage variables begin to take on more importance.

The State of Iowa Writing Project and similar projects are prime examples of extended in-service experiences. For three weeks, twenty-five elementary and secondary level teachers are involved in collaborative learning, which succeeds because the whole range of presage variables is modeled by the facilitators. One-shot in-service sessions can look impressive, but in longer intensive staff development experiences, the participants can focus on substantive learning, rather than on impressions of learning. In successful workshops, the teachers learn new behaviors rather than merely collect recipes for classroom practices.

Context Variables

The contexts in which in-service and staff development sessions take place are varied. In-service education is meaningless, however, unless it addresses teachers' specific needs and purposes. In-service education is clearly important in the development of a practicing teacher's abilities. Orlich (1983) has described five modes in which training can be offered:

> 1. JOB-IMBEDDED. The job-imbedded mode allows teachers to learn while actually on the job. . . .
> 2. JOB-RELATED. This contextual mode often takes the form of workshops where teachers work together with resource people to solve a problem of interest to the group. . . .
> 3. CREDENTIAL-ORIENTED. The credential-oriented mode is used mainly by those seeking advanced certificates or degrees. . . .
> 4. THE PROFESSIONAL ORGANIZATION-RELATED APPROACH. Advocates of this idea perceive teachers as professionals— willing and able to diagnose their own needs for in-service training and then to design and conduct that training. . . .

5. THE SELF-DIRECTED MODE. The final concept views teachers and self-motivated professionals who are interested in maintaining
and improving their own skills through reading, self-directed research
and other self-initiated activities. (199)

The motivation involved in any of the five modes naturally differs a
great deal from teacher to teacher. The job-imbedded mode may depend
upon the climate of the school or district as much as any of the other
modes do. If the administration, other staff, and the community are
concerned with maintaining a perceived status quo, a teacher's learning
will tend to be minimal under this mode. On the other hand, if teachers
are encouraged by the administration, other staff, and the community to
study teaching approaches actively and to seek out the most effective
means of working with students, then the job-imbedded mode of teacher
learning will thrive. Good teaching is, after all, carrying on research by
carefully observing the constant flow of data in one's own classroom and
dealing professionally with those data. Teachers who have experienced
learning in in-service sessions will make the most use of the job-imbedded
mode.

In its worst state, the job-related mode is most often typified by in-
service sessions at the beginning of the year, when all staff members hear
the same speech from a "motivational speaker." At its best, job-related
in-service education grows out of needs that teachers perceive in a
supportive school environment and that can be addressed in various ways
during the school year. Some commonly used methods are early dismiss-
als, late starts, released time using substitutes, and teacher-to-teacher
support, such as the coaching concept in McRel's Effective Schools
Program (see Joyce and Showers 1982) and Hunter's (1983) script-taping
conferences.

The last three modes are not tied directly to the school setting, but
they do suggest a need for a working environment where advanced
degrees, professional organization activities, and self-directed study are
recognized and rewarded. Teacher improvement or change that can lead
to the increased effectiveness of schools is directly related to the context
in which teachers function. Teachers who receive no encouragement for
learning and experimenting with ways to improve student learning find it
difficult to sustain themselves and to have any interest in degree programs.

Process-Product Variables

The question of what effect in-service training has on teachers has been
dealt with primarily on a superficial level in the research to date.
Typically, this research takes one of three forms:

1. An investigation into whether teachers liked the in-service session. Usually these data are gathered by questionnaire immediately following the session, and no follow-up investigation is expected.

2. A follow-up study that takes place long enough afterwards to give participants a chance to use the teaching strategies presented during the session. In such investigations, a program is considered successful if the teachers are still using the strategies at the time of the follow-up study. Typically, data are gathered by mailed questionnaire.

3. Research that considers teachers' reactions to the workshop, continued use of the strategies presented, and—perhaps most importantly—the effect of these strategies on student attitudes and achievement. Much more attention is given here to personal contact and interviews with teachers. The purpose is to determine not only the process teachers have gone through in implementing the concepts and skills gained from the session, but also the effect on students in the teachers' classes.

The investigations related to the first form of in-service evaluation range from questions about the comfort of the participants to what they felt they had gained from the sessions. "Satisfaction" questionnaires have no implied follow-up beyond the session, and it is unlikely that they would detect substantial change in a teacher. Obviously, the total erosion of any change made in the participants as a result of the session would go unnoticed even a day later.

One of the most extensively used examples of the second form of in-service research (investigating the extent to which the in-service strategies are being used) is the Concerns-Based Adoption Model (CBAM). The CBAM is based on the assumption that change is a lengthy, complex, and highly personal experience, and that implementation can be accomplished only when the different needs of teachers are met as they emerge. In "Evaluation of Staff Development: How Do You Know It Took?" Loucks and Melle (1982) share their beliefs about staff development evaluation as those beliefs have evolved from the use of the CBAM model:

1. The "proof of the pudding" for staff development efforts aimed at helping teachers develop new skills and/or use new practices lies in *whether those practices are then used in the classroom.*

2. The only way to find out about change in classroom practice is to *interact individually with each teacher* to find out.

3. Evaluations are only good *if they are useful,* and can directly contribute to further improvement in teachers and schools. (114–15)

When done effectively and consistently, follow-ups can result in much greater success for in-service and staff development efforts.

The third form of research cited above is beginning to receive increased attention. The job-imbedded in-service mode typically includes this third form. The Bay Area Writing Project, the National Writing Project, the State of Iowa Writing Project, the Colorado Writing Project, and others are showing that in-service training is carrying over into improving student writing. These projects are successful largely because the teacher learning experiences integrate substance, skills, and process. Hunter (1975) reports:

> When teachers learn to deliberately and consciously incorporate the essential "nutrients of learning" in their daily planning and teaching-learning interactions, and when the Teacher Appraisal Instrument is used to diagnose and prescribe for increased teaching excellence, we have found marked increases in students' self-concept, learning achievement, and teacher satisfaction. This increase has been vali-dated in pre-service education programs, in-service education pro-grams, and in elementary and secondary inner city schools with minority students. While our work is in its infancy and many aspects need further research, it is a robust infant with great promise for making successful learning and teaching satisfaction more predictable and more probable than ever before. (6)

With investigations of classroom effects from in-service training at least under way, some attention must be given to whether in-service education of any kind can help change the "less successful" teachers. To what extent does teaching experience "set" teacher behaviors? Are these behaviors (teacher properties) more difficult to change or easier to change after teaching experience than they are in a pre-service setting? When in-service education is related to clear-cut outcomes and when the follow-up is immediate, there seems to be some promise that change can be effected.

Lawrence (1974), examining ninety-seven studies of continuing edu-cation of employed teachers, found that 80 percent of the studies reported significant changes in teacher behavior. Lawrence goes on to point out that "the findings seem to confirm the generalization that 'you get what you train for,' so long as the gain is made relatively soon after the training." Yarger, Howey, and Joyce (1979) reached a similar conclusion about in-service participants' preference for "more direct in-classroom follow-up immediately after initial training."

If in-service training is to be an effective force in changing teacher behaviors and student learning, constant attention must be given to effective and efficient follow-up.

Summary

The Dunkin and Biddle variables and the organic field model of the teaching of English, which is explained in this monograph, promise to be valuable ways of studying in-service teacher training in English. The assumption that in-service and staff development will, in some mystical way, have an effect on teacher attitudes and student achievement must be questioned. If the relevant variables were consciously brought to bear on each trainer-to-teacher encounter, it is highly likely that much more efficient use would be made of English language arts in-service and staff development time.

References

Bethe, L. J., and S. M. Hord. April 1981. A Case Study of Change: Inservice Teachers in a National Science Foundation Environmental Science Education Program. Paper presented at the annual meeting of the American Educational Research Association, Los Angeles. ED 200 589.

Dunkin, M. J., and B. J. Biddle. 1974. *The Study of Teaching*. New York: Holt, Rinehart and Winston.

Graves, D., and V. Stuart. 1985. *Write from the Start*. New York: E. P. Dutton.

Hall, G. E., R. C. Wallace, and W. F. Dossett. 1973. *A Development of Conceptualization of the Adoption Process within Educational Institutions*. Austin: Development Center for Teacher Education. ED 095 126.

Haugen, N. S. March 1982. An Investigation of the Impact of the Wisconsin Writing Project on Student Composition. Paper presented at the annual meeting of the American Educational Research Association, New York. ED 214 203.

Hunter, M. 1975. The invariants of successful teaching. *Telemetry* 3 (3): 5–7. Los Angeles: UCLA Graduate School of Education.

————. 1983. Script Taping: An Essential Supervisory Tool. *Educational Leadership* 41 (3): 43.

Joyce, B., and B. Showers. 1982. The Coaching of Teaching. *Educational Leadership* 40 (1): 4–10.

Lawrence, G. December 1974. *Patterns of Effective In-Service Education*. Tallahassee: State of Florida Department of Education. ED 176 424.

Loucks, S. F., and M. Melle. 1982. Evaluation of Staff Development: How Do You Know It Took? *The Journal of Staff Development* 3 (1): 102–17.

Naftulin, D. H., J. E. Ware, Jr., and F. A. Donnelly. 1973. The Doctor Fox Lecture: A Paradigm of Educational Seduction. *Journal of Medical Education* 48:630–35.

Olson, M. C., and P. DiStefano. 1980. Describing and Testing the Effectiveness of a Contemporary Model for In-service Education in Teaching Composition. *English Education* 12:69–76.

Orlich, D. C. 1983. Some Considerations for Effective In-Service Education. *The Clearing House* 56:197–202.

Patton, M. Q. 1982. Reflections on Evaluating Staff Development: The View from an Iron Car. *The Journal of Staff Development* 3 (1): 6–24.

Ryans, D. G. 1960. *Characteristics of Teachers: Their Description, Comparison, and Appraisal.* Washington, D.C.: American Council of Education.

Yarger, S. J., K. R. Howey, and B. R. Joyce. 1979. *Inservice Teacher Education.* Palo Alto, Calif.: Booksend Laboratory.

Contributors

Faye Louise Grindstaff is a professor of education at California State University, Northridge. She has served as president of both the Southland Council of Teachers of English (Los Angeles) and the California Association of Teachers of English. She is currently on the Executive Board of the Conference on English Education and is a member of the Commission on Research in Teacher Effectiveness. She is the author of *Exploring Literature* and has made presentations at NCTE and CATE on teaching effectiveness and methodology in teaching English.

Richard Hanzelka is Language Arts and Staff Development Consultant for the Mississippi Bend Area Education Agency. He is a member of the Iowa Writing Project Steering Committee and served as vice-chair of the Iowa Department of Education Committee, which recently published A Guide to Curriculum Development in Language Arts. Hanzelka has also served on a number of NCTE committees related to curriculum, research, and teacher certification.

Miles C. Olson is a professor of English education at the University of Colorado at Boulder. He directs the Colorado Writing Project, an affiliate of the National Writing Project. Olson is senior author of The Writing Process, a series of texts for use in secondary schools. He has been heavily involved in the assessment of student writing abilities, having established the first statewide norm for Colorado students in grades 7 through the college freshman level. He is widely published in the area of writing assessment. The quality of his teaching and scholarship has been recognized by his students and his peers through the Teaching Recognition Award and the 1987 Distinguished Faculty Award.

William H. Peters is a professor of English education and head of the Department of Educational Curriculum and Instruction at Texas A&M University. He is chair of the Conference on English Education Commission on Research in Teacher Effectiveness, and his primary areas of research interest focus on effective teaching theories and practices and on the relationship between teacher behaviors and student learning outcomes. His research and writings have appeared in Research in the Teaching of English, The Journal of Educational Research, English Education, The Journal of Teacher Education, and other professional journals.